E-MAIL
SELLING
TECHNIQUES

(That Really Work!)

Stephan Schiffman
America's #1 Corporate Sales Trainer

BUSINESS

Avon, Massachusetts

Published by Adams Media, an F+W Publications Company
57 Littlefield Street, Avon, MA 02322
www.adamsmedia.com

ISBN 10: 1-59337-744-4
ISBN 13: 978-1-59337-744-1

Printed in the United States of America.

J I H G F E D C B A

Library of Congress Cataloging-in-Publication Data
Schiffman, Stephan.
E-mail selling techniques / Stephan Schiffman.
p. cm.
Includes index.
ISBN-13: 978-1-59337-744-1
ISBN-10: 1-59337-744-4
1. Internet marketing. 2. Electronic mail systems. 3. Selling—Data process-
ing. I. Title. II. Title: Email selling techniques.

HF5415.1265.S347 2007
658.8'72—dc22
2006028133

This publication is designed to provide accurate and authoritative information
with regard to the subject matter covered. It is sold with the understanding that
the publisher is not engaged in rendering legal, accounting, or other professional
advice. If legal advice or other expert assistance is required, the services of a
competent professional person should be sought.

—From a *Declaration of Principles* jointly adopted by a Committee of the
American Bar Association and a Committee of Publishers and Associations

Many of the designations used by manufacturers and sellers to distinguish their
products are claimed as trademarks. Where those designations appear in this
book and Adams Media was aware of a trademark claim, the designations have
been printed with initial capital letters.

This book is available at quantity discounts for bulk purchases.
For information, please call 1-800-289-0963.

To all who ever believed in the dream.

Contents

Part Three: What Works

Part Four: What Not to Do

Acknowledgments

This book is a compilation of concepts and principles developed over a long period of time, and I would be remiss if I neglected to mention the following people, each of whom made important contributions to the material between these two covers. My profound gratitude goes out to: Larry Shea, Scott Forman, David Rivera, Alan Koval, and Ben Alpert; Jim Levine, Daniel Greenberg, and Stephanie Kip Rostan at the Levine Greenberg Agency; and Gary Krebs and Shoshanna Grossman at Adams Media. Of course, my deepest gratitude goes out, as always, to Daniele, Jennifer, and Anne.

Introduction

I knew for sure that technology had changed the selling landscape forever when I started getting requests from unknown salespeople begging me to review the e-mail messages that they had created to send to key prospects. There was nothing particularly surprising about receiving anonymous requests from readers. For well over a decade, I had gotten calls and letters from salespeople asking for my help in critiquing traditional aspects of the selling process: the calling approach, the proposal, even the cover letter that was meant to thank a prospect for showing up for a face-to-face meeting. Then, almost without warning, in the late 1990s, I started getting a different kind of request.

All the other appeals were still there, of course. I still had plenty of calling approaches, proposals, and thank-you letters to look over in what I laughingly referred to as my "spare time." (You don't really get much of that when you run a global sales training organization, it turns out.) But in addition to those documents, people started asking me how to create a compelling e-mail headline, how to create text that people wouldn't scroll past, and how to avoid problems with spam filters.

It was all very flattering, of course . . . and it was also a bit of a challenge. Back in 1998, which is about the time I remember these questions starting to come in, we hadn't yet developed a systematic approach to resolving any of these questions. It was about then that I realized we had some work to do, because we ourselves were making mistakes in these areas that were costing our company business.

What you're holding in your hands right now is the result of eight years of ongoing discussions with my readers, my company's clients, and my staff on the best answers to the tough questions that the era of e-mail communications technology has been throwing at salespeople with ever-increasing urgency—and will no doubt continue to throw our way. An ever-growing share of the salesperson's day is devoted to creating, critiquing, and sending e-mail messages; perhaps a few years down the line, some fresh change in technology will inspire me to write a new book about a new series of questions. (Maybe everyone will communicate by means of iPods at that stage; I wouldn't be surprised.)

For now, this book is the very latest and most reliable information I have been able to assemble on the subject of e-mail, a communications tool that has caused more than one "expert" to adjust some of our core assumptions about selling. In the twenty-first century, the world of business is a great deal smaller and faster than it was even at the end of the twentieth, and for better or for worse, a big part of the reason for that is on display when you and I check our e-mail accounts. Here's hoping the advice that follows—all based on direct experience—comes in handy at some point before that crucial moment we hit "send."

I'd love to hear your opinion about what follows. Please share your impressions by writing to me at *contactus@dei-sales.com*. I really will do my best to answer you. And who knows . . . you may inspire another book!

Stephan Schiffman
New York City

Part One

Foundation Concepts

Chapter 1

A Tale of Two E-mail Messages

Once upon a time there were two e-mail messages. The first looked like this:

Subject: Our implementation notes and related items

Good morning Mr. Miller:

I am Mike Conway, Senior Sales Associate for ABC Interactive Media, located here in New York City. I would like to have the opportunity to share with you some notes on assessment and implementation that we have assembled by means of a careful review of the existing prospective customer base that overlaps with your industry, a copy of which list is available in a variety of different formats for your review. We understand that you are a major manufacturer of widgets, and we wish to make you aware that we have a significant number of widget plants and widget-related businesses on our current customer list, all of whom have come to rely on us for widget retooling services. (One of these is Century Manufacturing, a supplier of yours whose operations manager, Ken Steiner, suggested that I give you a call.) You will find more information on this on our company's Web site, www.retooler. org, which is accessible and fully functional via both Microsoft Outlook and Mozilla Firefox. To access the list of companies with whom we have worked, simply access the site and click on the function bar that reads "client list," then work your way through the first fifteen categories until you reach the sixteenth one, which reads "Widget companies with whom we have worked." At that point, you will be able to click the icon and access the names of the firms in question. These, just to clarify, are the firms I wish to discuss with you in person. May I ask that you phone me as soon as possible at 606-555-5555 to discuss the possibility of our evaluating this list together?

Yours very sincerely,
Mike Conway

P.S. I would like to assure you that our client references are of the highest possible quality and that I can give you my personal assurance that you will not be disappointed by a decision to contact me by telephone, which I hope you will do at your earliest possible convenience.

Here's what the second e-mail message looked like:

Subject: Ken Steiner

Ken, as you know, works for Century Manufacturing, one of our clients; he suggested that you and I meet to discuss your widget retooling plans for the coming year.
　　　Could we meet this coming Tuesday at 2:00 P.M. at your office?

Sincerely,
Mike Conway
www.retooler.org
978-555-0555 (office)
978-555-5550 (cell)
978-555-5050 (home)

Which e-mail message would you be more likely to read? Which e-mail message would you be most likely to respond to? If you were the CEO, which e-mail message would you be more likely to forward to your administrative assistants with the note "Set up a meeting with this guy?"

Chapter 2

E-mail and the
New Sales Culture

E-mail has made it easier for salespeople to communicate than ever before.

That's both a good thing and a bad thing.

It's a good thing because I, a salesperson just like you, can now contact virtually anyone in the world. For the first time in history, I can reach out to a prospect or customer and send that person a message that reaches them in just a few seconds.

It's a bad thing because I can also *screw up* that conversation in a millisecond.

The new sales culture, at least where e-mail is concerned, is one that is all too often based on instant actions, on rambling away, hitting "send," and seeing what happens next.

In the case of the two e-mails you just read, hitting "send" in the first example is a great way to make sure the person never opens another of your messages for the rest of his life. (I'll go further—it's a great way to make sure the person never even takes your call— assuming that he remembers your name from the long e-mail that you sent.)

By the way, did you notice how the one piece of information that the reader might conceivably have a positive reaction to—Ken Steiner—was buried in the middle of the message, where it was least likely to be read by a busy executive?

Notice, though, that in the second e-mail, that single piece of relevant information was in the subject line . . . the very first thing our executive (or whoever is screening his incoming e-mail) would be likely to see. Notice, too, that the second message didn't take all day to answer the reader's unspoken question ("What the heck do you want?").

Our sales culture may be priming us to hit "send" to as many prospects and customers as possible . . . but if our job is selling (and since you're reading this book, I'm assuming that your job is selling), we have a duty to increase the odds that the people we're trying to communicate with will actually open, read, and take action on the e-mail messages we send. If they do that, we will accelerate our sales process.

That's what this book is all about.

Chapter 3

Way Back When

When I first started out as a professional salesperson, more years ago than I care to remember, there was not only no such thing as e-mail—there was no such thing as a personal computer.

You could pretty much count on every piece of communication falling into one of two categories: People were either talking to you face to face, or they *weren't* talking to you face to face.

Nowadays, they may well talk to you face to face once, then conduct the rest of the relationship by means of e-mail messages and conference calls.

You're used to that. And I'm used to that. Now. Back in the 1970s, though, most of the important interaction would come about as a result of these quaint things we used to call "meetings." That's an old, out-of-date term, I know—let me define it for you. By "meetings," I mean situations where you and the prospect or customer could sit down, face to face, and talk things over. With *nothing else going on in the background.*

A wild idea, I know, but believe it or not, that's actually how we used to do business. People would say, "Hey, I'm going into a meeting, hold my calls, please." And then they would walk, with the salesperson, into a room without (gasp) any access to the Internet whatsoever! And then, having ushered the salesperson to his or her seat, the person you were talking to that day would actually stride over to the door, *close it*, and focus on you, and only you, for 30, 60, 90, sometimes even 120 straight minutes!

Yes, that was how it was back in the covered-wagon days of the Carter administration. It's a little embarrassing to admit that I was in fact alive back then, but the truth is, I was.

Meetings are still the lifeblood of the field sales force. They are not important for people who sell over the telephone, of course, but for those of use who still sell face to face, the advent of e-mail has profoundly changed the dynamic of the selling relationship. In some ways, it's made it much more difficult for us to sell in 2007 than it was for us to sell in 1977.

How, specifically? (That's not a hypothetical question. I'd really like to ask you to think of your best answer before moving on to the next chapter.)

Chapter 4

The Information Equation

I just asked you how, specifically, the selling job is likely to be more difficult in 2007 than it was in 1977. I hope you came up with an answer of your own. Here's my answer. Compare it to yours and see how close we are.

Back in 1977, if you bought from me, you and I had a series of face-to-face meetings where I was pretty much the only thing happening in your world for a half-hour or so at a time.

In the twenty-first century, if you buy from me, I'm lucky if I get any one-on-one time with you, and during our (brief) face-to-face encounters, there are usually a whole lot of other things happening.

SCENARIO A: In 1977, I would ask you for a meeting, and you would either meet with me or you wouldn't. If you did, we would meet face to face, I would suggest another meeting, and you would either give me that one or not, and then eventually I would close the deal with you—perhaps after three or four face-to-face sessions.

SCENARIO B: Nowadays the cycle (in some industries, at least) might very well look like this:

- You e-mail me based on something you saw on my Web site.
- I e-mail you back asking for your phone number so we can chat.
- You e-mail me the telephone number and let me know the best time to reach you.
- I pick up the telephone and call you but reach your voice mail system. (This is another piece of technology that was not around when I first started selling. But I digress.)
- You return my call and we actually speak, voice to voice. (Note that this is the point at which the relationship might have actually begun thirty years ago.)
- We agree to meet a week from now on Tuesday at 2:00.

- We do in fact meet face to face, and we have a good discussion about how we might be able to work together. I ask you for another meeting, and you agree that we should talk again this time a conference call that involves your boss (who operates out of another city) and a member of your technical team.
- We set the date and time for that conference call.
- I try to confirm the conference call by sending everyone an e-mail message a few days before we are scheduled to "meet."
- You and the others acknowledge receipt of your e-mail message. But there's a scheduling problem.
- We set up another time that works for everyone.
- I confirm the date and time of the conference call once again, and this time everyone's schedule is in agreement.
- We have the conference call, and we all discuss how we might be able to work together. You agree that it sounds good, and you ask me to draw up a formal proposal. We set a date and time for another conference call.
- I work up the proposal.
- I confirm the date and time of the conference call.
- Once again, the timing doesn't work, and we have to reschedule.
- I reconfirm the date and time of the conference call.
- This time everyone is on the call. I go over the proposal point by point, and you love it. You ask me to draw up a contract.

Obviously, there are big differences between Scenario A and Scenario B. The main disadvantage of Scenario B in comparison with Scenario A, though, is that I have much less time with anyone face to face.

That's an extremely important fact, and one that's potentially quite damaging to me, the salesperson, because of something I call *the Information Equation*.

The Information Equation sounds like this:

The quality of the information I, the salesperson, get from you, the prospect, tends to improve with the number and quality of our face-to-face interactions.

Please read it again before you move forward in this book!

Chapter 5

The Information Equation, Continued

The quality of the information I, the salesperson, get from you, the prospect, tends to improve with the number and quality of our face-to-face interactions.

When I explain this Information Equation principle to salespeople during our training sessions, they instantly "get it," and my bet is that if you've been selling for more than six weeks or so, you "got it" after reading the words twice in a row.

When I (the salesperson) meet with you (the prospect) in person, not just once, but for a second or third or fourth time, the quality of the information you share with me tends to get better. It's a reliable principle. People really do share things with salespeople they have back in for another meeting that they don't share on the first meeting.

And guess what? The quality of the information gets even better if the meetings you agree to have with me take place in different venues. First, you let me sit down in your office. Then, a week later, you walk me through your factory. Then, a week after that, you introduce me to your boss and show me her office. What I learn from you on that third visit is, as a general rule, going to be more meaningful on that *third* face-to-face visit than the information I got on the very *first* face-to-face visit.

That's just a universal principle of human relations as it applies to the sales process. You may occasionally run into an exception, but I guarantee you that in *most* of the situations where you have meetings with people, the information improves with the number of face-to-face meetings you have.

Now look again at Scenario B in the previous chapter, and you will notice that *our business culture is moving away from face-to-face meetings and toward remote meetings.*

This trend seems likely to continue, which means that if you do nothing and simply keep setting up conference calls as instructed, the quality of the information you get from your customers and prospects is going to decrease over time, and you're going to close less business.

In fact, if you're like most of the salespeople I train, you can very easily think of situations where you played Scenario B through for weeks or months on end . . . and then lost the business for mysterious reasons that became clear only after the fact. You know what happened? Someone else was getting meetings while you were settling for conference calls. Someone else was building relationships while you were reconfirming people's schedules.

So—what do we do about that?

Chapter 6

Wishful Thinking

Here's what we don't do. We don't spend all day writing e-mails designed to get us into more conference calls when we could be finding ways to get in front of more people face to face.

I wish I could tell you that the act of writing a better "let's have a conference call" e-mail message than your competition will, in and of itself, guarantee you a better relationship with, and better information from, your prospect.

But I can't.

If I were to tell you that, I would be engaging in wishful thinking rather than strategic thinking. And wishful thinking, alas, is the one syndrome I have identified over the years that has inevitably led to failure among individual salespeople and organizations as a whole.

Here's what I can tell you. If you're smart, and if you implement the principles in this book, you can use e-mail more intelligently than your competition is currently using it, and thus get *more in-person meetings* and *accelerate your selling cycle*. In so doing, you will improve the quality of your relationship—and thus improve the quality of your information and your likelihood of closing the deal with people who keep moving forward through the sales process with you.

Ultimately, I think you should be using e-mail as a tool to establish momentum with people who could conceivably buy from you. And I'm going to warn you ahead of time, if your job is to sell face to face, you're going to get the best results if you use e-mail to uncover reasons to get face to face with your prospects and customers.

If you sell over the telephone, your goal is going to be to have as many good conversations as possible with your prospects. The best way to do this is to establish commitments for a "phone appointment," as in, "Yes, I will agree to talk to you again tomorrow at 2:00 p.m." You must, unfortunately, accept as a fact of life that someone who manages to establish a face-to-face relationship with your customer, while you can maintain only a voice-to-voice relationship, is very likely to steal the account away from you. In any event, most of what follows in this book about using e-mail to support the sales process will be very easy for you to adapt to the telesales world. (See also my book *Stephan Schiffman's Telesales*.)

To understand what I'm talking about, you have to have a little bit of background on what can go wrong in the selling process. Let's look at that more closely right now.

Chapter 7

Screwing Up the Sales Process

One of the interesting things about the twenty-first-century sales process pattern that I called Scenario B is that it features many more possible "touches" with our contacts than Scenario A did. It also exposes us to more people than Scenario A did.

I'm not saying those facts are good or bad, just that they're worth understanding. They're part of the new selling environment we all face today. If we understand that environment and act intelligently in response to it, we will prosper. If we don't, we won't prosper.

So: You want more "touches"—or at least the opportunity for more "touches"—and more contact with more people within the purchasing organization. By "touch" I mean something that I, the salesperson, do to remind you that (a) I exist, and (b) you and I have a relationship that could be beneficial to you.

Back when I first started selling, there were only three ways to "touch" a contact: mail the person something, call the person on the telephone, or meet in person.

Now we have this technology that makes it much, much easier to "touch" the person to whom we are trying to sell. But notice that a meaningful "touch" takes place only *after* I have already established some kind of relationship with the person. In other words, it is no good fooling myself into thinking that I am "touching" a sales prospect, or improving the relationship in any way, if my pattern looks like the following sequence, which I'll call Scenario C, or "The Scenario That Screws Up the Sales Process":

- I e-mail you and ask you for a meeting, even though you have never heard of me before.
- I e-mail you again the next day, asking why you did not reply to my earlier e-mail message.

- I e-mail you again on the third day asking what I have done wrong and why you would ignore so many messages in a row.
- I go on your Web site and find your telephone number.
- I reach out to you by telephone—for the very first time—and leave you a voice mail message asking if you have gotten my e-mails.
- A week after that, I e-mail you again, reminding you of all the messages you have been ignoring, and suggesting that you be so polite as to call me so that we can set up a meeting.
- The following day I repeat the request, under the pretext that you may have missed my earlier phone message.
- The day after that I send yet another e-mail message that includes the text of all my previous e-mail messages to you. I once again request that we have a face-to-face meeting.
- Three months go by. I don't contact you during that time. Amazingly, you don't reach out to me, either.
- After that three-month period has elapsed, I e-mail you again and ask once again for a face-to-face meeting. The process begins all over again.

Obviously, the "touch" in this sequence is very different from the "touch" in the sequence that resulted in you actually buying from me.

In Scenario C, *there is no relationship*. There is no buy-in, no connection, and certainly no conviction on your part that you will benefit in any way, shape, or form by granting me your (divided) attention for fifteen minutes.

Let's be realistic. In Scenario C, I do not even have any guarantee that you know that I exist—much less that you have read my messages. And considering the possibility that my e-mail messages may have been blocked by your company's mail system, there is really no way for me to be certain that you ever could have received my messages!

If I'm committed to Scenario C, complete with that telling three-month gap, I'm committed to either bugging you to death or ignoring you completely.

Truth in advertising disclosure: There is no e-mail strategy you can employ—nothing outlined in this book or in any other book—that can possibly overcome the damage you can do by making Scenario C your default selling routine. Can you use e-mail to initiate a productive relationship with someone?

Sure.

Can you *obsess* with e-mail and thereby initiate a productive relationship with someone? Sorry, no.

Let me tell you a story that illustrates what I mean. There was a guy awhile back who stumbled across my company's Web site and "decided" that he was going to become my business partner. Did he call me (or e-mail me) to ask for a meeting so we could discuss this potentially huge step, in person? No. He blizzarded me with "ideas," day after day after day, as though the fact that he had my e-mail address meant he *already* had a business relationship with me. He didn't. I got every newsletter, every article, every quote, every media mention this person could muster. And I got literally dozens of personal e-mail messages from him. There was this massive wave of e-mail that I was supposed to read (or maybe memorize) based on . . . let's see . . . *nothing* that he and I had ever agreed to do together.

You know what my first reaction was when I heard that he was on the phone and wanted to talk to me?

"Not the crazy e-mail guy!"

You know what my reaction would have been if he had left a voice mail message on the same day, asking for a conference call with me, him, and one of his people?

"Not the crazy e-mail guy!"

You know what my answer is now if anyone, anywhere, asks me what I'm looking for in a business partner?

"Not the crazy e-mail guy!"

Chapter 8

Relationship = Commitment

Any meaningful business relationship is built on the principle of commitment.

As salespeople, we get little commitments first—like "Yes, I'll agree to meet with you," or "Yes, I'll take your call on Tuesday at 8:00 A.M." And we build our way up to more meaningful commitments—like "Yes, I'll give you a tour of our plant," and "Yes, I'll introduce you to my boss."

Along the way we gather information, and if we're lucky, that information improves in quality and depth over time. Why? Because we've made suggestions about things we could do together that are

- Perceived as helpful to the other person
- Easy for the other person to agree to

I want to ask you to take a very close look at those two criteria. They're extremely important for anyone who actually wants to practice and implement e-mail selling techniques that really accelerate the sales process, as opposed to e-mail selling techniques that constitute wishful thinking.

Let's say I want to get a commitment from you to buy from me. I can't do that without the right information from your side. Agreed? The information you give me, if I do my job right, should improve in quality and depth as time passes.

Well, that will only happen if I suggest things to you that are (all together, now):

- Perceived by you as helpful
- Easy for you to agree to

If my suggestions meet those criteria, we may—*may*—end up doing business together.

If my suggestions don't meet those criteria, we definitely—*definitely*—will not end up doing business together.

You've just read the basic philosophy I'm going to ask you to apply, not only to all your e-mail messages with prospects and customers, but to all your communications of any kind, and in any medium whatsoever, that involve prospects and customers.

Chapter 9

No Magic Wand

Granted: E-mail really does give salespeople the opportunity to have more frequent, and more widely distributed, contact with more prospects and customers than I ever dreamed possible back in the mid-1970s. At the same time, e-mail is a trap.

It's a trap because we, as salespeople, are often sorely tempted to consider the medium of e-mail to be more of a "magic wand" than it actually is, or can be. We want to write some snazzy copy, wave the e-mail wand, hit "send," and make hordes of willing customers appear. To my mind, that's not selling, but rather order taking. And it's not what this book about.

E-mail is a tool for moving a relationship forward, and a very good tool. It is not the best tool for *initiating* a relationship, although it can serve this purpose occasionally. Not very often, though, in my experience. (When was the last time you actually built up a meaningful business relationship based on an e-mail you received from somebody you did not know?)

The vast majority of the blind e-mails that I get I automatically delete. My guess is that you do the same. So it would be both dishonest and impractical, in my view, for us to pretend that blind e-mails are really the answer to the array of selling challenges that most field salespeople and telesales professionals face.

Sending out huge volumes of blind e-mail isn't the answer, and most salespeople I run into already understand this (even though some marketers have tried implementing the blind e-mail approach on a large scale).

The reality is this: E-mail is part of your tool kit. If you are incapable of communicating effectively with your prospects and customers by means of e-mail, you are probably not going to do very well as a professional salesperson in today's marketplace. These days, salespeople simply can't say, "I'm not comfortable using e-mail." It's a little bit like saying you don't feel comfortable talking with your prospects and customers on the telephone. If you were to say that, you would be granting a huge competitive advantage to everyone who competes against your company and goes to bed at night dreaming of turning *your* customers into *their* customers.

So in that sense we really are looking at a radically different selling environment. We can no longer say, "I'm just not good with computers; don't bother me about e-mail." But at the same time, some salespeople are under the impression that they can e-mail their way *around* the task of making cold calls or networking at public events in order to generate leads. And I think that's just as big a mistake.

Believe me when I say that I know how tempting it is to believe that e-mail has rendered prospecting obsolete. After all, nobody really enjoys making cold calls, and we're always on the lookout for evidence that some technological advance has rendered obsolete something we really don't like to do. But the sad truth of the matter is that even superior, seasoned, experienced salespeople find themselves in an income crisis when they neglect prospecting for extensive periods of time. That was true in 1977. It's true in 2007. And I will bet you my fifty-dollar bill against any box of doughnuts you choose that it's going to be true in 2037.

So my first and overriding message to you is this one: Learn how to use e-mail to support your sales process—but do not expect e-mail to replace the prospecting that is a natural part of your sales process.

Chapter 10

This Won't Hurt a Bit

The truth of what I just told you can only be demonstrated by sharing a little bit from my own experience. If you have ever seen me deliver a live program, or read one of my books, the odds are very good that you will be familiar with some of what follows. Even so, I am going to ask you to read the following paragraphs.

It's important information to learn and reinforce, and I promise it won't hurt a bit to make your way through the next few pages.

Every day that I am not training, I make fifteen dials. When I say "dial," I am talking about a revenue-generating attempt that involves picking up the telephone, dialing the phone number of a business that could conceivably use my services, and hearing another human being answer the phone. It is important to notice that the fifteen dials are all different dials—they are not the same dials to the same people I called yesterday, nor are they fifteen attempts to reach the same person in a single day. Out of those fifteen dials, I will generate, on average, seven "completed calls." What is a completed call? That's a call where I speak to somebody who could decide to give me a meeting to discuss the possibility of working together. The designation of a completed call varies from company to company, but the basic idea is this: If you reach only the receptionist, and the receptionist is not whom you want to have the meeting with, even a "good conversation" with him or her is not a completed call. If you are trying to reach the VP of Sales, and the VP of Sales *is* whom you want to have the meeting with, then that is a completed call, whether the conversation lasts four seconds or two minutes. Notice that the completed call does not have to result in the person agreeing to meet with me—it just has to result in a *discussion about* whether to meet me at a particular, scheduled point in time.

Now, then. Out of those seven completed calls, I will typically schedule one first appointment. That means that one of those seven discussions results not only in my asking, "Hey, can we get together this coming Tuesday at 2:00?" but also in the person on the other line agreeing that it does in fact make sense to meet with me this coming Tuesday at 2:00. That is a first appointment—or "FA." Look again at how it breaks down numerically.

15—7—1

If I do that every day, I will schedule a total of five first appointments—but first appointments are not the only kind of meeting I will invest my time in with my prospects and customers. There are also follow-up meetings. After all, if I make these calls every day and if my selling cycle takes more than one visit—which it does—then a certain amount of my week may be taken up with discussions involving people I spoke to last week, who agreed to meet with me again this week.

As it happens, the actual number of total visits that I go on, first appointments plus follow-up visits, is eight—and of those eight personal visits I go on each and every week, approximately one will turn into a sale.

15—7—1
8—1

Let's assume that I keep that up for an entire year, with two weeks off for vacation. That means fifty weeks, which means I make a total of fifty new sales as a result of all that activity.

Now, here's the big question: Why do I make those fifteen dials each and every morning? If you were in one of my training programs and you answered something to the effect of "Because that is the right number for you in terms of your yearly income goal," you would be absolutely right. You would get a gold star. In fact, I do not just make those fifteen dials every day because there is nothing better that I can think of to do, or even because anyone else told me to make fifteen dials. I certainly do not make those dials because I enjoy the process of making unsolicited calls to total strangers. No, the reason that I make those fifteen dials each and every day is that I want to generate those fifty pieces of business at the conclusion of the year.

I know that, given my ratios, I need those fifteen dials in order to generate the fifty new pieces of business, which is my yearly target. I realize that all these ratios connect to one another; the fifteen dials to the seven completed calls; the seven completed calls to the 1 appointment; the eight visits to the average 1 sale, and the fifty sales a year arising out of everything that came before it.

That really is my lifestyle number, those fifty new deals a year. And the only way I can make it happen is to make fifteen dials a day.

The question you may be asking at this stage of the discussion is, What on earth does this have to do with e-mail messages? And the answer is—plenty. To the degree that I try to use e-mail to replace those fifteen dials I have to make each day, I'm messing up my sales process. Bitter experience has shown me that I am going to depress those ratios if I take the dials down. I will not be more effective by attempting to create a relationship by means of initiating contact through e-mail. I will only become less effective. You can challenge me on this. You can share your own stories about e-mail prospecting, and I hope you will. But the past ten years of research both in terms of my own selling activity and the selling activity of literally tens of thousands of salespeople all leads me to believe that even though e-mail is a tremendous tool for improving the quality of an existing relationship, it is generally a lousy tool for initiating relationships with people who don't know about your company.

If I still make the fifteen dials a day, and I use e-mail creatively and intelligently on top of that activity, I may be able to improve my other ratios. But not if I skip the dials.

If you feel differently, then I have to be honest and tell you that this may not be the book for you. In this book, we are going to be learning how to use e-mail as an effective selling tool, but in order to do that we have to understand and accept the principle that e-mail messages sent by individual salespeople are, by and large, not effective relationship-creation tools.

I go into the topic of setting first appointments in my book *Cold Calling Techniques (That Really Work!)*. I also have included, as an appendix to this book, a brief overview of the telephone-prospecting process that you may find helpful. But my point here is that in this book I am giving you tools that you can use to accelerate or expand or maximize the potential of an existing relationship. I am not going to make you the promise that most salespeople want me to make, which is that selling becomes easier when you eliminate cold calls and replace them with some sophisticated e-mail campaign. That simply is not the case, and I don't think I would be doing you any favors if I implied that it were the case.

Chapter 11

Mass E-mail
Ticks People Off

I mentioned a little earlier that attempting to use huge volumes of blind (that is, unsolicited) e-mail to create or initiate a relationship is a mistake.

Making this your central prospecting strategy might seem like a good idea at first. After all . . . the process seems simple and straightforward enough, doesn't it? Buy a blind list, write a message, blast 40,000 people at a time, wait for the fan mail and inquiries to come back.

In fact, there are a whole bunch of reasons for you *not* to do this.

The first and most important reason is that you are a professional salesperson, and a professional salesperson is, by definition, someone who is focused on the development of personal relationships. Making vast numbers of anonymous, remote, identical appeals is what a billboard does, not what a salesperson does.

I should say, too, that my personal experience indicates that mass e-mail *lengthens* your selling cycle rather than shortening it. It also *increases* the amount of time you have to spend doing boring, fundamentally unproductive things like dropping people's e-mail addresses from your list.

There is, in addition, one more great reason not to use mass e-mail as your primary strategy for developing new relationships with prospects. It is this: Doing this invariably gets a certain percentage of people really, really furious.

Now, don't misunderstand me. There are plenty of businesses built on the principle that it makes a whole lot of sense to send out thousands (or even millions) of unsolicited, unauthorized e-mail messages every single day. I'm not saying those companies don't exist. What I am saying, though, is that those businesses are, quite frequently, operating one step ahead of a pack of furious e-mail recipients—people who have gotten so sick and tired of (a) receiving stuff they didn't ask for, and (b) having to delete all that junk that they do things like call their senator, the Federal Trade Commission, and, for all I know, the Knights of Columbus in order to complain. Not surprisingly, a fair percentage of the businesses we are talking about are also operating one step ahead of the sheriff.

The federal government has passed important and far-reaching legislation that severely limits the nature of unsolicited e-mail that a business or a person representing a business—that is, *you*—can send out. The legislation is called CAN-SPAM, and its stated goal is to reduce the seemingly overwhelming tidal wave of unsolicited e-mail with which virtually everyone who uses a computer nowadays is already all too familiar.

By the way, did you know that the use of the term *spam* to describe seemingly ceaseless waves of unsolicited e-mail was inspired by a (pre-Internet) skit created by the British comedy troupe Monty Python? Did you know that the skit ridiculed the Hormel Company's (still-popular) smoked ham product by repeating its name in a man-tralike incantation, with minor, numbing, and now iconic variations as part of a surrealistically obsessive restaurant menu? Did you know that the Hormel Company has somehow come to terms with all of this, and has launched a Web site allowing you to join the "Spam Fan Club" online? Did you know that you have to opt in to the list in order to receive e-mail about Spam, the product? Did you realize that by requiring you to volunteer your e-mail address in exchange for an online fan club newsletter, the Hormel Company thus secures permission to send out marketing e-mail to what is known as an "opt-in" list, and is thus following sound and accepted corporate practice, and avoiding forever the accusation, too terrible to contemplate, that it sends people spam about Spam? You did know all that? Well, then, never mind.

Be honest. You yourself are no fan of the spam that you receive from people who try to sell you various prescription medications or car insurance deals, not to mention steamier or perhaps less ethical business propositions that may come your way by means of spam. Think, then, about how angry a prospective customer (or an actual client!) might be upon receiving a similarly unsolicited e-mail message from you or your company.

I will assume that you are reading this book because you want to do business responsibly, promote a positive image of your company, and create and sustain responsible business relationships that benefit both parties. Sending out waves of unsolicited e-mail is simply not the way to do any of these things.

Rest assured that there is a way to engage with prospects and customers using e-mail and that we will be looking at these methods in detail in the next chapter of this book. (Hint: It has something in common with the e-mail messages the Hormel Company sends members of its "Spam Fan Club.")

For now, I want to share with you, for the sake of thoroughness, the key points of the federal legislation limiting unsolicited e-mail. Take a good long look at these guidelines—and make absolutely sure, as you implement the ideas in this book, that you and your organization are following them to the letter.

Ten Things You Should Know about CAN-SPAM

1. CAN-SPAM applies only to commercial e-mail.
2. CAN-SPAM applies to e-mail for which a primary purpose is to feature your goods, services, or content even if you do not send the e-mail yourself; however . . .
3. CAN-SPAM does not apply to third-party advertisers who advertise in your mailings.
4. CAN-SPAM can apply to e-mail sent out by your affiliates on your behalf; however . . .
5. CAN-SPAM will not apply to e-mail sent out by your affiliates on your behalf unless you know, or should know, that the e-mail is being sent in violation of CAN-SPAM and you stand to gain from it financially, and you don't try to stop it.
6. CAN-SPAM requires that all information in your e-mail headers and body be true, accurate, and not misleading.
7. CAN-SPAM requires you to provide a fully functioning means of return Internet-based communication for the purpose of the recipient opting-out of your mailings.
8. CAN-SPAM requires you to honor those opt-out requests, and to immediately cease sharing the user's address even with previously agreed-to partners.

9. CAN-SPAM does not require that you use confirmed opt-in for your mailings; however, it is one of the best defenses against an accusation of CAN-SPAM violation.

10. CAN-SPAM does not require ISPs to accept e-mail that is CAN-SPAM compliant. In fact, ISPs are specifically exempted from claims that they must accept e-mail if it complies with CAN-SPAM.

[This list is reprinted with permission from the Institute for Spam and Internet Public Policy from the eBook *CANSPAM and You: E-mailing Within the Law,* by Anne P. Mitchell, which is available at *www.isipp.com/can-spam-and-you.php.* Copyright ©2004, Anne P. Mitchell. For more information please contact *info@isipp.com.*]

By the way, "ISPs" are Internet Service Providers (like AOL).

A "confirmed opt-in" mailing list is defined by the good people at EmailLabs (*www.emaillabs.com*) as "a two-step process to allow a user to opt in to your list. They must (a) initially sign up, and then (b) respond to a follow-up e-mail to confirm their opt-in to your mailing list." If you think about it, you'll realize that most of the marketing e-mail you *actually pay attention to* comes to you after you have completed both of these steps with some organization—in exchange for some kind of intellectual content you initially receive from that organization.

Chapter 12

What Makes E-mail Different

There are, of course, lots of ways that e-mail differs from other methods of communication, but the chief distinction I want you to bear in mind is that e-mail is, at its foundation, remarkably easy to ignore.

In fact, it is so easy to ignore that people routinely get in trouble for ignoring it!

The tide of e-mail we each have to do battle with these days is so vast and covers so many possible topics and is presented in so many different environments that we often miss extremely important e-mail messages from people we are striving mightily to impress!

Isn't that true in your world?

Think back on your own workplace relationships. At some point within the last year, haven't you accidentally overlooked a really critical e-mail that a customer, a prospect, your sales manager, the CEO of your company, or maybe even a member of your family sent along? Didn't you, at some point during the past year, have to make an excuse like the following: "I am so, so sorry I missed your e-mail—I was working on yada yada yada, and I did not notice that your message had come in. Please forgive me."

What about times when you even forgot to acknowledge a message from one of these important people that was marked *urgent* or had a red flag next to it? Has that ever happened? Ouch!

If you're like me, and the vast majority of people who write and read business e-mails, you have in fact missed important e-mails from customers, clients, or other important business allies—even though you did not mean to.

So what does this mean for us as salespeople? Well, for a start, it means that we should build in an assumption that a lot of our e-mail is going to go unread.

Yep. You read right. The odds are quite good that the person *will not* read your message. This is one reason that I am not a big proponent of spending hours and hours crafting the single most perfect e-mail message possible for somebody who does not yet know, or may not remember, that I exist. If this person may well, without meaning to, ignore a message from his mom, there is a decent chance that my message is going to get ignored, too. I'm not saying we should never send a message to such a person, mind you, only that we should recognize that sending it is, in basketball parlance, a low-percentage shot.

But there is another implication, one that I want to share with you here, that I think too many salespeople lose sight of:

We gain absolutely nothing by reminding people that they have missed or ignored our e-mail. And in fact we only do ourselves a disservice when we do this.

Chapter 13

What Makes E-mail Different, Continued

When I train salespeople to improve their sales process, I appeal to something that I call the three universal communication principles.

In order to prove to you that it really is a huge strategic mistake to remind a prospect or customer that he or she forgot to open your e-mail, or missed something you said in it, at any point, ever, I want to share those principles with you right now.

Principle #1 is this: *People respond in kind and we control the flow.* These are basically two sides of the same coin. "People respond in kind" means that if I walk into a roomful of people and give everyone a high-five, I'm going to get a certain, predictable response from the people in that room, a response based somehow on what I've just done. I could expect a much different response if I were to walk into a room and, as my first communication with the group, ask in a really loud voice, "What the hell is wrong with you people? How come you can't follow basic instructions from your own sales manager?" In the first instance there is going to be, in all likelihood, a very positive robust, energetic response—and in the second example there is going to be a dead silence, one that is probably going to send the rest of my training program with that group into the shadow of the valley of death. So we really do control the flow, and people really do respond in kind to what we say or write.

The second principle is as follows: *All responses can be anticipated.* By this I mean that it is not going to be a surprise to me when people respond in certain ways to the consistent messages that I send over a period of months or years or even decades as a salesperson. I have made thousands upon thousands upon thousands of telephone prospecting calls during the course of my career. It is not exactly earth-shattering news to me that, during one of those calls, someone I have reached out to is likely to say to me, "Steve, I am really not interested at all in this." In fact, because I know that that response is likely to come up, I can strategize for it and develop a response of my own, because I have more practice with handling that kind of conversation than the other person has in responding to it. (Specifically, I can say "You know what, that's exactly what ABC Company—my very best customer—said when I first tried to meet with them. I really do think we ought to meet. Could we get together on Tuesday at 2:00?")

The third principle is equally straightforward: *People communicate through stories.* That means that I can tell that the relationship is really moving forward when you share a story with me about how you made a certain decision; by the same token, I can enhance the possibility of the relationship moving forward in this way if I tell you a story that is relevant to your situation. This is a basic principle of human interaction: Once we find a narrative for something, and we identify with that narrative, we are more connected to the person who shared it with us.

Now then—why have I shared all this with you? Because there is a disease among salespeople in the United States and around the world. Millions upon uncounted millions of salespeople initiate conversations with a question that sounds like the following:

"Hey, do you remember getting the e-mail that I sent along about blah blah blah?"

Stop!

Be honest. How eager would *you* be to answer this question?

At the end of a long day, or perhaps the beginning of a new one, how eager would you really be to get a call from me asking you whether you remembered receiving an e-mail message from me?

Start from the most obvious entry point. Statistically speaking, what are the odds that you actually do remember *any* e-mail message from somebody who is not a customer, colleague, or superior of yours? Pretty low, right?

So what do we gain by opening a conversation in this way?

Nothing. In fact, in doing so, we violate the guiding ideas behind all three of the principles about communication.

Look at communication principle #1: We control the flow. What kind of flow do we choose by asking the person, "Do you remember my e-mail?" Well, we have chosen a "flow" that is almost certainly going to cause the other person to tense up and feel defensive. We have gone out of our way to choose a topic that he or she will almost certainly be unable to answer in a positive way, and one that is not likely to move the conversation forward constructively. We are asking the other person to admit that he or she has made a mistake and confirm the (statistical likelihood) that he or she does not remember or ignored our earlier message.

Not a great dynamic for the conversation.

How is the person going to respond? Look again at communication principle #1. The person is going to respond in kind. He or she is going to address the subject we've raised, not some other subject. So that means the person is probably going to find some way to suggest that the reason that he or she does not remember opening the e-mail message is that it was missent or mislabeled, or that things were too busy for him or her to get to that message. At the very least, we can rest assured that these kinds of responses are going to flash through the person's mind. What we may get in terms of actual dialogue is a stony silence or some effort to change the subject or simply get off the phone.

How about principle #2—all responses can be anticipated? How does opening the call in this way measure up there?

Let me answer that question by posing another one. How many hundreds of times, how many thousands of times, do salespeople have to open a conversation with a question like "Do you remember getting my e-mail?" to realize that the response they are going to get is rarely, if ever, going to be a positive one? I should think five or ten ought to be enough. If, after ten straight times, you notice that this question does not yield a great rapport once you ask it of a prospect or customer, you can assume that this very same dynamic is going to play the next time you choose to open a conversation with it.

Now let's look at the third piece: People communicate via stories. Does asking this question encourage people to tell the story? Sure it does. Here is the kind of story that it is likely to generate:

"Once upon a time, there was a great reason for me not to remember you, your e-mail message, or your company. Actually, there were several dozen reasons. For instance, my boss was mad at me about missing a deadline; our best customer went off to a competitor. The government is regulating us in all kinds of interesting and unexpected ways. And then, in and among all those crises, you sent me an e-mail message. I could go on and on. Listen, you have no idea how busy I was yesterday. I have absolutely no way to keep track of all the things that are hurtling through my life. So there are dozens, maybe hundreds, of reasons that I cannot be expected to remember, much less read, e-mail messages from strangers, and in fact cannot ever meet with you to discuss your company. Frankly, I now realize, to my horror, that I have a meeting in a couple of minutes with no time whatsoever to spare for this call. That was the way things went yesterday. And that is pretty much the way things are today. Goodbye." Click.

You get my point. The only "story" we are likely to elicit here is one that reinforces a narrative that is already quite well established—namely, that the person does not have time to talk to us.

So instead of asking people whether they remember receiving your e-mail, whether they read your e-mail, whether they opened your e-mail, or whether they drew any conclusions about your e-mail, my suggestion is that you open the conversation with something entirely different—something that has nothing whatsoever to do with whether the person had access to or remembers or connected with your e-mail message. For instance:

"Hi, Jim. This is Steve Schiffman from DEI Management Group. I had some ideas that I want to share with you about improving the efficiency of your sales force the next quarter, and I wanted to drop by tomorrow afternoon at 2:00 and discuss them. Is that a good time for you?"

We are not badgering the person about whether he remembers the e-mail message that we sent. We are simply re-emerging on his or her radar screen, giving some kind of context, and suggesting what should happen next. That is it.

If that discussion brings up the fact that he saw the e-mail, liked it or did not like it, so much the better. But the flow of the conversation will be stronger if we make the discussion about a topic that we *want* to engage in—namely, whether a meeting was going to take place—as opposed to a topic that we *do not* want to engage in—namely, whether the person remembers receiving our e-mail message.

Chapter 14

Why E-mail Is Not Enough

I've seen a lot of "brilliant new e-mail approaches to sales" over the past few years. They usually have to do with prospecting. The prospecting plans take lots of different paths, but they tend to have these two things in common.

- They never involve actual discussions with strangers.
- They do involve sending out lots of e-mail.

Every single time one of these schemes is submitted for my approval, I try to talk the person out of building his or her whole quarter, month, or week around the plan. To explain why, I have to give you some background.

According to the breakthrough work of Howard Gardner in his book *Frames of Mind*, human beings have seven distinct levels of intelligence. We all function on all seven of these levels, not one, and we function at different degrees in each of those seven intelligences. Given this, the idea that a single IQ test can accurately evaluate human intelligence is simply absurd.

Based on this concept, it turns out that e-mail correspondence neglects vast chunks of the human intellectual system. In fact, it appeals directly to only a couple of the intelligences Dr. Gardner identifies. Let me outline them for you now so you can see exactly what I'm talking about.

Gardner identifies the following specific intelligences. As you read what follows, remember that we *all* have these intelligences; we're just not all equally brilliant in all seven.

1. *Verbal and linguistic intelligence.* This has to do with how one uses language. People who are born writers are gifted in this area of intelligence. Clearly, verbal and linguistic intelligence is part of what happens when you compose a positive and

compelling e-mail message. For people who are very "good with words," the act of composing, reading, and responding to e-mail messages takes advantage of this type of intelligence. People who have extraordinary verbal or linguistic intelligence can also communicate effectively by listening, by speaking, by reading, by writing, and by making connections between concepts and ideas they identify in different sources. Important: It is possible (and quite common) for someone who has great verbal skills not to be a particularly good reader or writer; such a person might be incapable of responding effectively to an e-mail but would be better attuned to a telephone conversation.

2. *Musical and rhythmic intelligence.* Gardner identifies a rhythmic sense in which some people excel and others do not. He identifies people with high intelligence in this second area as extremely sensitive to the musical elements of pitch, timbre (by which he means the characteristic markers of a given tone), and rhythm. To get your head around this level of intelligence, consider that even people who cannot hold a tune can still be moved by a powerful piece of music, or can find a commercial jingle compelling enough to recall it at various points throughout the day. When we do these things, we are using our musical and rhythmic intelligence, even though we ourselves may be poor musicians. Notice here that musical and rhythmic intelligence has nothing whatsoever to do with reading or responding to e-mail messages—unless, of course, (1) there is a sound file attached to the message, (2) the organization's spam blocker has not blocked the message because of the attachment, (3) the recipient decides to open the attachment—which is not at all a certainty, given the prevalence of concerns about viruses—and (4) the person has the software necessary to listen to the attachment. That's a lot of "ifs," so let's just say that the second variety of intelligence is not closely linked to receiving e-mail messages.

3. *Logical and mathematical intelligence.* People with high intelligence in this area have a passion for abstraction and a deep-seated need to explore and discover. They enjoy analyzing,

breaking down, and resolving problems. They may or may not be great at math, but they almost certainly have a lot in common with Sherlock Holmes. Those blessed with very high intelligence levels in this third area may take great pleasure in identifying inconsistencies or errors in reasoning that others have missed. Now, it is possible that somebody who employs this kind of intelligence may do so by means of an e-mail message. But notice that e-mail messages from this person are likely to be long, that they may require a great deal of technical understanding, and that they may identify more problems than opportunities. So even though this third level of intelligence does technically connect with a type of functioning relevant to the medium of e-mail, the resulting communication may not always move your sales process forward. To the contrary, the person with high-level logical and mathematical intelligence may delight in sending e-mail messages that identify new (and, often, insurmountable) obstacles for salespeople!

4. *Visual and spatial intelligence.* Here Gardner identifies the intelligence that allows people to understand visual reality. People who score high in this realm of intelligence know how to create, interpret, and transform visual images. They may think in terms of pictures. Inasmuch as salespeople must usually avoid incorporating visual imagery in the body of their e-mail messages, primarily for practical reasons (spam filters may pick up the image and keep the message from ever reaching its intended recipient), it's safe to say that the types of e-mail messages that we are primarily discussing in this book do not appeal to people who score high in this fourth realm of intelligence.

5. *Bodily and kinesthetic intelligence.* This variety of intelligence, according to Gardner, has to do with things one can do with one's body, and the fluency and grace necessary to execute physical movement. Bodily and kinesthetic intelligence takes the form of both highly sophisticated movement of the body, like that of a ballet dancer, and intricate manipulation of physical objects, like the work of a sculptor. Notice that in the example of a sculptor, the bodily and kinesthetic

intelligence compliments the visual and spatial intelligence. If it is your job to create a business relationship with someone whose most developed intelligence is bodily and kinesthetic, e-mail should not be your medium of choice. Think about it. Reading and responding to e-mail is essentially a sedentary activity. It might well be the polar opposite of bodily and kinesthetic intelligence—the kind of activity someone gifted in this area would be likely to go out of his or her way to avoid.

6. *Intrapersonal intelligence.* This kind of intelligence, familiar to anyone who has ever written a love letter or received one, has to do with expressing one's own feelings and perceptions. Consider the achievement of a great poet, raconteur, novelist, or playwright, and the potential of this unique intelligence area will become clear to you. Such people understand their own reactions and emotional patterns, interpret them effectively, and can even reproduce them or simulate them in a way that allows others to participate in them. Since research indicates that much human decision-making is driven by emotion rather than cold logical assessments, appealing to people's emotions—how they feel and why they feel that way—would seem to be a powerful and important sales strategy. Unfortunately, people with high levels of intrapersonal intelligence are sometimes strongly internally oriented, which means that they may need a strong personal bond with you before they even begin to evaluate your written message.

7. *Interpersonal intelligence.* This is not to be confused with intrapersonal intelligence, which, as we have seen, points toward the individual's own feelings and perceptions. Interpersonal intelligence, on the other hand, is pointed toward other people. People with high levels of interpersonal intelligence are often considered charismatic and powerful leaders. Here's the extraordinary thing about people who score high in intelligence level seven: They often intuitively understand, and adapt their communication styles to, people with high intelligence in any of the other six categories. Salespeople often score very high in the area of interpersonal intelligence (so

consider yourself lucky if this all sounds strangely familiar). Great politicians and great speakers may score high in this seventh level of intelligence; this is the "leadership intelligence." In general, this level of intelligence is the one that allows someone to "bond" powerfully with individuals or groups; somebody who has a "knack for dealing with people" is likely to have high levels of interpersonal intelligence. But here's the catch. If you are aiming to sell to somebody whose primary intelligence connects powerfully to human interaction, it is unlikely that you will want to base most (or any) of your initial contact with that person on an activity that requires him or her to stare at a computer screen.

You can see, I hope, that Gardner's system gives salespeople important new insights about the intelligences that are operating simultaneously within *all* of us—and on the importance of using different methods to connect with people based on that.

Now here's the part I want you to remember. If your strategy for uncovering new prospective customers relies solely on (or even primarily on) pointing them toward words you have written, words that can only be displayed on a computer screen, it seems likely to me that you will be missing huge chunks of the audience—and that missing that many people will be a mistake.

For some people—perhaps a majority of people—eye-to-eye, face-to-face, and/or voice-to-voice interaction will be an intrinsic part of their intelligence set. Interpreting (or even noticing) e-mail from strangers will feel, to them, like translating a foreign language.

Use e-mail as one of the tools in your outreach campaign, but be ready for in-person activity, too. You should be ready to engage in one-to-one linguistic and verbal exchanges; you should be ready to play a great piece of music or a powerfully cut video that uses music; you should be ready to prove your case with logical precision if necessary; you should be ready to use imagery during face-to-face presentations and in your organizations marketing materials; you should be ready to "walk around the plant" and allow a prospect to show you a physical location or demonstrate a product; you should be ready to ask a prospect how he or she feels about something, and be ready to *listen* to the answer; and you should be ready to allow somebody with a very high level of interpersonal intelligence to turn you into one of his or her audience members.

Mastering all seven of these intelligence skills, and *then* using e-mail intelligently to support the relationship, will move you forward in ways that relying on e-mail alone as a prospecting tool simply cannot.

Chapter 15

Top of the Mind

What is the single most pressing question on your mind when you evaluate whether to open an e-mail message? If you're like me, that question is "Do I really have to look at this?"

Now—why do we ask ourselves that question before we even open the message? For a very simple reason: You and I and everyone else in America with access to the Internet and an e-mail account are constantly struggling to keep track of a sea of e-mail messages, most of which are totally irrelevant to our world.

Our prospects and customers are in the same boat.

Even if we have the world's best spam filter, and even if we somehow manage to set our e-mail preferences in such a way as to prohibit messages from reaching us unless we actually know the person they're coming from, we are *still* likely to receive messages that have absolutely nothing whatsoever to do with us or our workday.

Why?

Because large numbers of people find it satisfying to "copy" just about everyone on earth with their own e-mail messages. Because the guiding principle in business communication today sounds something like this: When in doubt, copy somebody on the message. That seems to be the approach, doesn't it?

So between the commercial messages that we have absolutely no interest in and the latest update from the people in human resources on what they are having for lunch three weeks from now, we generally have far too much e-mail to keep track of—and too little time to keep track of it.

If that is an everyday reality for people in sales (and it is), we can rest assured that it is an everyday reality for the people you are trying to sell to. We have an overflowing inbox. So do our prospects and customers.

So why do so many salespeople assume that this is not the case? Why do they write e-mail messages that assume that people have all day long to read what they want to pass along? Why do they assume that the person who is evaluating the message has been waiting breathlessly to receive the latest update on what has just happened in the salesperson's world?

Our job is to increase the odds that our e-mail does not get lost in the shuffle. To do that, we have to make certain that we are putting *only* relevant information in front of the other person.

That's the driving principle. Make sure the information we convey by e-mail to our prospects and suspects features *only* relevant information. (A "prospect" is someone who's actively playing ball with us; a "suspect" is someone we want to sell to who *isn't yet* playing ball with us.)

These days, salespeople ask me at just about every training event whether, and how, they should use e-mail as a prospecting tool. As you have no doubt gathered by now, my feeling is that, because most unfamiliar e-mail messages are ignored, e-mail is simply no replacement for prospecting by phone. Therefore, it shouldn't distract you from prospecting by phone.

Even so, e-mail may occasionally be useful for reaching out to specific contacts with whom you otherwise couldn't connect. Some people really will react more quickly to an e-mail message than they will to a telephone call. And they will react positively—if the message reaches them in the first place, if they open the message, if the message has meaning for their day, and if the message is perceived as helpful. If you do all those things, the message will stand a decent chance of attaining what the marketing people call "top of the mind" awareness.

I believe that any e-mail you use to try to set up an initial meeting should be crafted in just the same way that the opening of a face-to-face sales meeting or discussion should be prepared: with skill, care, and foresight.

Let's look at some strategies for doing that now.

Chapter 16

Nine E-mail Strategies for Accelerating the Selling Cycle

Here are nine ways to increase the odds that the e-mail prospecting message you send will accelerate your selling cycle.

1. *Choose a heading that gets you noticed.* In the subject line, try using a reference name, someone you can list as a referring party or someone they might know. Consider referencing a company that will be familiar to the reader, one that you have worked with in the past. You can then build your message around your work with that company.
2. *Get to the point.* The message should be no more than two to three sentences long. The shorter it is, the more likely it is to be understood and acted upon.
3. *Use the person's name in the body of the message.* Otherwise, he or she may assume that this is an e-mail that a thousand other people are receiving.
4. *Emphasize commonality.* If you can, point out that your company has been doing business with other firms in this person's industry. Another way to emphasize commonality is to reference the name of someone you have in common, preferably in the subject line of the message.
5. *Don't try to sell.* Don't include long monologues about how great your company is. Say clearly that the reason for the e-mail message is to set up an appointment. Offer a specific time and date that you want to get together.
6. *Don't hound the person.* Send one message a week, maximum. If the person says she doesn't want to get any more e-mail messages, don't send any more messages.

7. *Don't make getting this particular individual to answer your message your life's work.* After three e-mail attempts, move on.

8. *Don't try to turn an appointment into a prolonged premeeting correspondence.* Once you have set the appointment, there is no need to turn the exchange into a protracted discussion. Send a polite, short message of thanks and confirmation and then show up at the appointed day and time.

9. *Include the name and the physical address of your company,* as well as a way for the recipient not to receive unsolicited messages in the future. This, as it happens, is a requirement by federal law.

Part Two

The Art of the Next Step

The Selling Process and the Next Step

My goal is to show you ways you can use e-mail to reduce your selling cycle, close more deals, and close bigger deals. But to do that, I have to break down some parts of the selling process in a little more detail.

You know why? Because doing things like closing bigger deals and shortening your sales cycle is what I call a "big picture" result. You have to be able to put a lot of little pictures together first. And specifically, you have to be ready to look closely at the concept of the Next Step.

Selling is a series of Next Steps.

When you ask someone to meet with you this coming Tuesday at 2:00, you are asking for a Next Step.

At the end of that meeting, when you ask the person to schedule another time to meet with you the following Tuesday at 1:00 so you can go over an idea, that is a Next Step.

When the person reviews your idea and says, "This sounds good. Let me talk about it with my boss." And you say, "I have an even better idea; why don't I introduce my boss to your boss? Could we do that this coming Monday at 1:00 p.m.?"—that, too, is asking for a Next Step.

If we get a Next Step, the sales process is moving forward. If we don't, it's not.

This concept sounds simple enough in the abstract, but it often proves quite difficult to apply to a specific situation.

When I am conducting sales-training programs, I will often run into salespeople who say that they understand this concept but actually show little or no evidence of familiarity with the concept of the Next Step. For instance, somebody in a training program will tell me that a prospect has a fifty-fifty chance of closing. I'll say, "That's great. Tell me—when you are next planning on talking to the person?"

And the answer will come: "Well, I don't really *know* when I'm talking to this person next, but probably at some point during the next month or so. Anyway, I really do have a good feeling about this sale."

The "good feeling" part is immaterial.

That relationship has no Next Step attached to it. That deal is, as a matter of statistical likelihood, highly unlikely to happen. (The statistics might *change* if you get the person to meet with you next week, of course, but that's not what we're talking about. We're talking about what the odds are right *now*.)

Chapter 18

The Best Available Evidence

It is a fact of sales life that people who are engaged with us, connected to us, interacting with us, and moving forward through the sales process with us don't mind agreeing to Next Steps with us. They are more likely to give us a spot on their calendar than other people. In fact, their willingness to connect with us at a particular date and time either in person or on the phone is the best available evidence of their willingness to move through the cycle with us, and, eventually, buy from us.

By the same token, someone's lack of willingness to give us a Next Step is *the best available evidence* that they will not buy from us.

The selling process that I teach breaks down into four steps. During training programs, I will mark the four steps off by showing four empty boxes, with arrows leading from one to the next. At that point of the program, I will ask the group this question: "If the sales process has four steps, what is the objective of the first step?"

I get a lot of different answers to that, answers like "Find out as much as you can about the person" and "Learn what the competition is like" and "Establish rapport" and even "Close the deal on the first meeting." Any number of things will come up. Someday, somebody's probably going to tell me that the objective of the first step is to do the Watusi with the prospect.

But the real answer to the question is much simpler than it first appears to the participants. In truth, the real objective of the first step of the sales process is simply to get to the Next Step.

That's it.

We have one and only one objective on the grand scale when we are talking about the sales process: make sure that it keeps moving forward. Insofar as that is true when we look at the whole sales process, it is also true to every substep within the sales process.

So if we were to break down those four boxes and identify them (as we'll do in the next chapter), we would see that they really do have distinct names and identifying characteristics. The final phase, of course, is the close. That is where the person agrees to buy from us. I prefer to think of it less as a close and more as a person deciding to *use* what we sell, preferably forever, at a profit to my organization. That's just a longer, slightly more accurate way of saying what most people mean when they use the shorthand expression "close," as in "to close the sale."

Here's the key question: What has to take place in our relationship with the prospect in order for the close to *happen?*

Chapter 19

What Has to Take Place?

We know that the fourth and final step of the sales process is the close. But let's look at the question from the last chapter again:

What has to take place in our relationship with the prospect in order for the close to *happen*?

Well, before the close there has to be some kind of a presentation or recommendation.

I'm using the word *presentation* here, but really what we are talking about is a *reason* for the other person to buy. We're talking about that *reason* showing up at the third step of the sales process, during the presentation. Let's work our way backwards, and look at the third and fourth steps of the sales process.

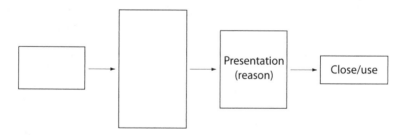

For the sale to close, there has to be a reason for the other person to say, "Yes, this really does make sense to me. I do want to use this."

And by the way, the discussion of that reason brings us to what has to be the world's simplest closing technique—namely, the "make sense" close. This is where we simply say to the prospect, "Gee, this really does make sense to me. I think we should get started. What do you think?"

In order for that to work, however—in order for the prospect to answer that question with a "yes"—there really does have to be a good reason behind the presentation, a reason that really does make sense to the other person. So, how do we determine which of all the possible reasons is in fact the reason that does makes sense for them to buy from us? Well, we have to gather information. And that is the portion of the sales process that comes right before the presentation phase.

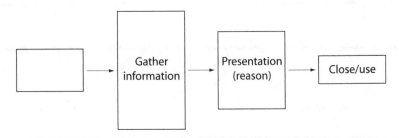

We make a point of emphasizing in our training programs that this information phase really does occupy a huge amount of the time and effort and energy that has to go into any meaningful sales process. There's a very good reason why this second box is the largest of the four shown. In fact, the objective is to spend 75 percent of your time in the sale gathering information from the prospect and verifying that information. Three-quarters of the time and energy that you invest in the sale has to come before you even make a presentation or recommendation.

This brings us to the next question: What makes that kind of information gathering possible?

Chapter 20

Establishing the Relationship

Obviously, I cannot just walk in the room and start shooting off questions; the prospect and I have to establish some kind of a relationship. There really must be some kind of give-and-take, eye-to-eye or voice-to-voice contact with the other person before we start imagining that we can move through the sales process and gather the information we need. So that is what our first step of the process is really all about, the opening of the relationship. This is where we are going to connect, do a little bit of building commonality and establishing some rapport with the other person. Obviously, we cannot gather any more information until we have actually done that.

So here is what we are looking at; this is the four-step sales process with all the labels identifying each of the steps.

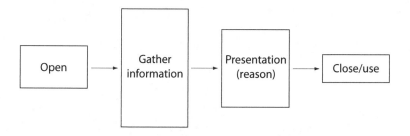

So what does all this have to do with e-mail? Well, the point is that once we make the effort and invest the time to sit down face to face with a person and open up the relationship, once we get to that first step, we can hasten the progress as we make our way through the other three steps by means of e-mail. We can stay on the person's radar screen, remind her or him of certain key points from previous conversations, even get the prospect involved in circulating our message to other important people in the organization, thus involving other players to help us expand our influence and access within the sale.

Once we have established the relationship, we can accelerate the sale, and e-mail is a good tool for doing that. The people we are talking to can help us move the sale forward more quickly because we can stay in contact with them not only through face-to-face and voice communications, but in a very direct way by means of tactful, nonharassing e-mail messages. I'm talking about e-mail messages that say, basically, "I'm still here, and we're still working together to make X happen for you."

This is basically e-mail selling by *staying on the radar screen*.

E-mail, in my experience, is not always a great tool for *getting* salespeople on the radar screen. (There are some ways you can use e-mail to get on the radar screen, but you can't build your whole prospecting strategy around e-mail.)

E-mail can be a superb tool for *staying* on the radar screen.

And, just as a reality check, we salespeople should acknowledge that a period of one-sided or noncommittal e-mail correspondence with someone may be a sign that we aren't quite as big a dot on the radar screen as we may imagine ourselves to be.

Chapter 21

Selling Signals and Buying Signals

This is a book about using e-mail to move your sales process forward. In light of that, and in light of the Next Step concept that we've been discussing, I want to address the question of what, exactly, does and doesn't constitute a "buying signal" during your interactions with customers, prospects, and clients.

Can you guess what a real "buying signal" is, in my world? Considering what we've been talking about for the past few chapters, I hope so. If the person is willing to commit to give you a chunk of his or her time at a specific date within the next two weeks, and does so in such a way that it actually makes it likely for you to move forward with this sale within your average selling cycle, then that really is an *actual buying signal*. Everything—and I do mean everything—else is a *fake buying signal*.

So, let's say that your average selling cycle is close to mine, which is eight weeks. And let's say that, this morning, you receive an e-mail from Jim Somebody, whom you have spoken to in the past—perhaps in a face-to-face discussion at a seminar, perhaps via the telephone, perhaps by means of a previous piece of e-mail correspondence. And let's say that in that e-mail message you receive, Jim Somebody agrees to your request for a chunk of his time and is willing to sit down with you for a meeting next Monday at 2:00. This will be his first commitment to you.

That is a buying signal.

It's not the *final* buying signal, of course. You could be talking to somebody who simply loves to meet with salespeople and has nothing else to do to fill his or her day. There are such people, just as there are people who enjoy rejecting salespeople out of some strange sadistic impulse to see them squirm during meetings. Could you spend weeks or months preparing a proposal for such a person? Sure you could. In fact, I'd be willing to wager that you probably *have* spent weeks or months preparing a proposal for such a person, and that you never managed to move forward to anybody else in the operation!

So you would have to be on the lookout during your meeting with Jim Somebody for *another* buying signal at the end of that initial meeting. If you get one, he's a prospect, in the truest (and only meaningful) sense of that word. There is a realistic prospect that he will buy from you. If you don't get a buying signal, *Jim Somebody is not a prospect.*

Specifically, you will be on the lookout for not just any buying signal, but a buying signal from Jim Somebody that *does not conflict with your typical selling cycle.*

By "not conflict," I mean that the buying signal should be connected not only to a specific date and time, but also, in some clear way, to what *usually* happens after the first meeting when you're dealing with people who end up actually buying from you.

For example, if Jim Somebody gives you access to his IT people at the end of the first meeting, and that access is something you typically need in order to move toward a proposal that eventually gets discussed at a second or third meeting, that's a buying signal. (If, on the other hand, Jim Somebody didn't give you access to his IT people for fourteen weeks, and you typically get access to them by the third week, then you are not looking at a buying signal, even though Jim Somebody may keep feeding you face-to-face appointments for all that time.)

Basically, we simply want to avoid getting distracted by *fake* buying signals that sound like this:

- "The guy really likes what I had to say." (Unspoken: "But he won't meet with me again.")
- "The decision-maker was very engaged and enthusiastic." (Unspoken: "But he isn't returning my messages.")
- "The decision-maker sent me an e-mail message telling me that I should check in next week and set up a time for us to meet." (Unspoken: "But he said the same thing last week, and the week before that, and the week before that.")

All those responses—and any one of their thousands of possible variations—are really "not buying signals" rather than buying signals. They are, to use a "technical" term, *fake* expressions of interest.

Chapter 22

The Date

Anybody who's made it through adolescence knows what a fake expression of interest sounds like—and how much it actually means in the grand scheme of things.

We had a trainer once who made the point I'm getting at in this way:

"Assume I'm still in high school, and assume I want to ask the most attractive girl in school to go to the dance with me on Saturday night. And assume that she really wanted to go with someone else. Would she say, 'No, I won't go out with you' right out loud? Or would she say something like 'I'm washing my hair on Saturday night'?

"Unless she was a heartless sadist, she would probably try not to hurt my feelings, smile as politely as she could, and say the shampoo thing. Right?

"Right. But suppose that polite smile of hers fooled me. Suppose I took it for a different kind of smile. Suppose I just didn't get it. Suppose I thought she really *did* have to shampoo her hair that night, and suppose I came back the next week and asked her whether she would like to go with me to the movies on Tuesday night. What would she be likely to say then?

"Well, if she was still trying to be a nice person, and we have no reason to believe that she wouldn't be, she might say something like, 'You know what? I have to reorganize my sock drawer on Tuesday night.'

"Now, suppose I still didn't catch on. Suppose I keep asking, week after week. Finally, after maybe eight more weeks, the bitter truth is going to come out. She's going to make it absolutely clear to me. She's going to say something like 'Look, I'm sure you're a nice guy, but you don't seem to be grasping the point here in quite the way it needs to be grasped. When I told you I was washing my hair instead of being able to go to the dance with you on Saturday night, what I was really doing was saying *no*. And when I told you I was reorganizing my sock drawer on Tuesday night instead of going to the movies with you, what I was really doing was saying *no*. And when I came up with those eight equally creative reasons that I couldn't go out with you on the nights you asked about, I was really saying *no*. In fact, I will *never* go out with you. It doesn't matter how many times you ask, the answer simply isn't ever going to be *yes*. So not only are you wasting my time, you're also wasting your time. You should be asking somebody else."

Why am I telling you a story about a guy who can't get a girl to go out with him on a date? Because, too often, we salespeople wait to hear the actual word *no*. We should learn to understand that the person is coming up with a creative reason not to meet with us, not to give us access to his or her key people, not to give us feedback on what we've done, and that it is in fact a way of saying *no* without using the actual word.

In fact, if you think about it, the call or visit where the person looks you straight in the eye and says, "You know what? We absolutely can't work with you"—that discussion is the honest discussion. At least with that person you don't go back and spend eight weeks tweaking a proposal no one is ever going to read. The person who says, "Gee, this looks interesting. Let me show it to some people and get back to you" is the person you've got to think twice about investing your time and energy in.

Back to e-mail. What I want you to watch out for is the possibility that information may come to you via e-mail that is in fact a fake buying signal masquerading as a real buying signal.

Why, you may ask, do we have to bear this in mind about e-mail messages in particular?

Because e-mail is, by definition, an inherently impersonal medium. If you're a salesperson, you will find that it is used by people who would rather communicate with you in a way that does not require any investment of time, effort, emotion, or energy whatsoever. The message from someone who doesn't really want to talk to you might look like this:

Subject: Fascinating

Bill, thanks for coming by today. You've given me a lot to think about. No problem if I bounce your idea off some of the people around here, I hope?

Thanks for taking all those notes. Please e-mail your proposal ASAP to my assistant Sandi (*Sandi@acme-org*) and I will call you back as soon as we get some consensus. Also, I forgot to mention to you that I'm off to England next Friday for a couple of months. Hope to be in touch when I get back.

Best to you and the kids,
Milt W. Stopcallingme
VP of Everything

I hope you have gathered, from my definition of "buying signal," that this kind of e-mail is a clear violation of the Next Step standard. You should call Milt before he gets on the plane to England and try to *set a date* for the two of you to review the proposal he's planning to circulate on your behalf.

All too often, e-mail messages are camouflaged so as to *look like* buying signals. Here's another example.

Subject: Link?

Thanks for your e-mail message. Can you e-mail me a link to your product list so I can take a look at what you have to offer?

Milt W. Stopcallingme
VP of Everything

That might sound like somebody who is actively engaged in figuring out whether it makes sense to work with you. But in fact, as with the previous message, there is actually no commitment whatsoever.

So what do you do? Of course you cannot refuse to let the person look at your Web site.

As a practical matter all you can do is comply with his request and briefly suggest something at the end of your message that *you* are going to do at some point in the next two weeks. For instance:

Subject: Re: Link

Thanks so much for your recent message; below is the link you requested.

 www.ourcompany.com/productlist

 I am going to be in your area on Tuesday morning at 10:00 meeting with the ABC Company. Why don't I stop by at 11:00 and meet some of your tech people?

Brenda Nextstep

This kind of request for a Next Step should become second nature to you in your e-mail messages. Some people will say yes. Most people will say no. And that's okay! You want to know who's really saying no to you.

Do it!

There is absolutely no excuse for not asking for some kind of future time commitment from the person with whom you are trying to build a relationship.

Asking is what salespeople do for a living!

In fact, you can rest assured that this person you are corresponding with knows that asking for such commitment is in fact something that salespeople do on a regular basis. So there is not going to be any hostility as a result of you making this suggestion, either via e-mail or in person. To the contrary, there is probably going to be a more direct and more authentic exchange of information than you might otherwise get. You are either going to get one of these two messages:

"Thanks for the suggestion, Tim, but we are really not ready to sit down yet. Do me a favor and give me a call around the first of February so we can try and set something up then."

Or:

"That sounds fine, Tim, but I have only fifteen minutes or so to spare. If you're willing to work with that, I can introduce you to some of our key people around here during that period."

Obviously, that is a buying signal. It is distinguishable from a "not buying signal" because—you guessed it—the person is actually taking a piece of his or her calendar and giving you access to it.

Suppose you get that first message instead? That is no problem. We call this kind of lead an opportunity. It is not a prospect. It is simply an opportunity for future business. Mark it in your tickler file or whatever other mechanism you have to remind yourself that this person asked you to get back in touch on such and such a date—and set up a meeting. Then call or e-mail without apology around that date, and suggest that you get together on February 7 at 10:00 A.M.

See what happens!

Chapter 23

"Hey, Would You Take a Look at My Web Site?"

It should go without saying—but I will say it anyway. Suggesting that the person visit your Web site and then get back to you to let you know what he or she thinks of it is not a great strategy for moving the sales process forward.

I get this all the time, usually from people I don't know who phone me and e-mail me and who are trying to establish some kind of first contact. "Hey, let me give you my Web site address. I want to know what you think of it."

This is basically the same as requesting that the person read your brochure and then give you a call to let you know his or her thoughts about it. If you can beat quota by doing that, my hat is off to you, but I suspect that neither you nor any other salesperson on earth can pull off that trick.

We want the call to go well. We want the e-mail message to produce something. We want to be liked by the decision-maker to whom we just reached out. So we make a huge mistake.

We want so desperately to think that we are satisfying the other person that we sometimes fall back into the habit of not challenging the prospect in any way. That's the huge mistake. "Oh, I'm not asking you to actually *do* anything meaningful in this relationship—just, in your off hours, of which I know you must have plenty, to review my brochure—er, Web site—and tell me what you think of it."

This common sales mistake loses sight of the fact that there *has to be some kind of creative tension in any selling relationship.* If the prospect is already happy doing exactly what he or she is doing right now, that person would have no need to talk to a salesperson. We, as salespeople, have to challenge our prospects' conception of what they are doing right now; we have to learn what they're doing right now and shake things up a little bit. We think it is possible that there may be a match between what we do and what they do. We think that the match may have aspects of value that they have not previously considered.

If none of this were true, our job description would not read "salesperson." It would read "order taker."

No, you don't want to overwhelm the person. At the same time, you don't want to fall into the trap of avoiding any possible tension in the exchange.

Ask *directly* for a *meaningful* Next Step. Instead of saying or writing, "Why don't you take a look at our Web site and then e-mail me back," call and say this, either directly or by means of a voice mail message:

"I came across an article that I want to e-mail you; it is a link that shows up on our Web site and it is a little hard to find. I am going send you the link because I think it has some good ideas for your blah blah blah initiative, and then I will call you tomorrow. I have some thoughts on how it might affect your business. I am planning on calling around 8:00. Talk to you then!"

Then send the article—as a link, not as an attachment. And call when you said you were going to call. Try to set a Next Step.

It's a pretty simple principle, but it's so easy for people to lose sight of it. Let's say that I am calling you to set an appointment, and you tell me that you are not interested in meeting with me. Well, you'll recall that I have a very specific response for that, one that I have worked out over countless prospecting calls, and it tends to have a pretty good statistical likelihood of at least continuing the conversation, and perhaps even moving forward to a scheduled first appointment. I say, "You know what? That's exactly what Joe Smith over at XYZ products told me, and now he's one of our best customers. Just out of curiosity . . ." (and then I ask a question).

I've trained salespeople on this stuff for over a quarter of a century. So can you imagine how it makes me feel when I get a prospecting call and I hear a salesperson say, "Hey, that's okay. Do me a favor. Jot down the name of my Web site and take a look at it and then let me know what you want to do."

I hang up instantly. This is the sort of thing that might make it sound as though some kind of meaningful discussion has taken place. But in fact, there is no discussion taking place. This is just a salesperson volunteering a "nonbuying signal" of his very own!

This suggestion provides absolutely no tension whatsoever in the relationship, and, as I pointed out, a certain healthy tension is essential to forward progress in the sales discussion. How do I know whether you could conceivably add value to my organization if you are not willing to make the case that you could?

How likely would you be to invest a chunk of your day reviewing the contents of a Web site based on a thirty-second discussion with a total stranger? Not very likely at all. So, if you are going to close the call with something, close it with an attempt to meet again or talk again or a suggestion about a way that you might be able to get face to face with the person at some public event. Do not issue meaningless and irrelevant suggestions that the person monitor your Web site. It is just not going to happen.

Chapter 24

The Message Template

Now I want to share with you a template for a basic format of an effective person-to-person e-mail message.

This is a good model—but not the only possible model. It's a sound approach to a "basic" e-mail message that focuses on a Next Step.

Notice that its subject line connects to a date that coincides with the Next Step that we want, and that the first line references a competitor or other company with which the recipient is familiar.

"Good" template:

Subject: Meeting on April 19
MAXWIDGET

We've done a lot of work for people in your industry, including MaxWidget. My boss suggested that you and I meet to discuss your widget retooling plans for the coming year.
 Could we meet April 19 at 2:00 P.M. at your office?

Sincerely,
Mike Conway
www.retooler.org
978-555-0555 (office)
978-555-5550 (cell)
978-555-5050 (home)
CONFIRMING APRIL 19TH MEETING AT 2:00 P.M.

The purpose of this message is simply to secure some type of involvement or Next Step or confirm an involvement or Next Step. There is absolutely no way anybody reading this message could misinterpret what it is about, get lost in a long paragraph, or misunderstand what kind of action is required or requested.

Notice, too, that the message can be read in full on a single computer screen display. As in, the person doesn't have to hit "page down."

The information at the beginning and end of the message is what is most important. If the reader is going to skip anything here, she is going to skip the material that shows up after the word *MaxWidget*. The human mind is trained to ignore what it does not process. By making an editorial decision to place the most important material at the beginning or end of the message, and by putting the least important information in the middle of the message, we are taking advantage of how the human mind works. All too often, people compose thoughtless e-mail messages where the most important information is buried in the middle of a long paragraph in a message like this.

"Bad" template:

Subject: Your skyrocketing profits

Your profits certainly will start to skyrocket once you realize that we've worked with some of the key people in your industry, including MaxWidget. That's why my boss suggested that you and I get together. What would be a good time for us to meet up? Maybe sometime next week? Let me know.

Mike Conway
Sales Associate
Retooler

See the difference?

The first message is the message I strongly suggest that you use as your model.

The second message is the message I want you to avoid like the plague. Dumb subject line. No Next Step request. Key information (the name of a competitor) buried in the middle of the text. No phone contact information. Nothing to catch the eye at the bottom of the screen. And even though it's quite short, it somehow seems long-winded.

Especially if you are still at the beginning of the relationship and still trying to secure some kind of initial commitment, the best advice is to keep your e-mail message short and make sure it follows the outline of the "good" template.

Follow the advice in this chapter to the letter, do so consistently, and then follow up your e-mail messages intelligently through other media, and I think you'll agree this chapter is among the most important in the whole book.

Chapter 25

The Perfect E-mail Message?

No, you don't have to send exactly the message I outlined in the previous chapter. Just follow the basic outline, and edit intelligently. Let's talk for just a moment about principles for making (minor) variations on the template you just saw.

The title of this chapter really does require a question mark at the end. There is no single perfect e-mail message that is applicable to all situations where we have the opportunity to move the sale cycle forward.

There is, however, a set of standards we can apply to most of the e-mail messages that go out to prospects when we hit "send." I want to share those with you now.

There are basically only three questions that we have to answer. They are:

- How long should the message be?
- How detailed should the message be?
- How casual should the message be?

I want to take you through these in order and share some thoughts on the types of answers that you should be giving as you create your messages.

Let us look at the first question: *How long should the message be?* The best answer is: pretty darned short.

As a general rule, the *only* people I will read long e-mail messages from are people who are either my customers or my blood relatives. When it comes to anyone else, I either skip the message entirely or read the beginning and the ending and decide from there what I should do.

Be honest. This is probably very similar to your own standard. My guess is that, in your world, the only people whose long messages do get read are those from your own customers, your boss, or relatives. (And let's be honest again: some of those messages from the people we are related to: We may not read every single solitary word of either.)

So. We're creating messages that we want people to read. It is incumbent on us to keep our messages short if we want to get anything accomplished by means of an e-mail message that moves the sales process forward. How short? Again, think in terms of a single computer screen.

Everybody who uses e-mail uses it in one of two ways these days: either by means of looking at a computer screen or by looking at a display that is considerably smaller, like a BlackBerry. That means that, more and more, those of us who write messages actually have a very small amount of space in which to make our point. For my money, it is best to keep the messages so short as to be impossible *not* to read if you glance at them.

I advocate an effective length of two to three sentences tops for the main portion of the message. Note that I am talking about the message that shows up in the body of the e-mail and not the subject line or the signature, which are separate animals.

Here's the second question. *How detailed should the message be?* The answer here is that the message should go into relevant detail and feature few of those details. For instance, if the message can emphasize that we have worked with a company in this prospective customer's industry, that is the level of detail we want to encourage—but we do not want to spend more than a sentence or three exploring that. We just want to mention the name of the company if we can and suggest what the person ought to do about it (usually, meet with us or talk to us).

In other words, we want our messages to be just as detailed as it takes to provoke curiosity and get a response—but no more detailed than that.

Let's look at the third question: *How casual should we be?* This is a very difficult question because the e-mail message has become, for so many of us, a replacement for verbal interaction. That means that during the course of our working day, if we are sending around e-mail messages internally, we may be tempted to adopt the same level of discourse that we would use if we were hanging around the water cooler. That would be a mistake. In fact, if we are reaching out to a brand-new person or someone we have only recently spoken to on the phone, we actually have to assume a somewhat higher standard.

You never know. You might run into a grammar cop, someone who will disengage from your message the moment he or she finds a minor writing error in it. (This is another reason to keep the message short, by the way—fewer possibilities for error.)

Consider the e-mail message to be a relatively formal document. (See also Chapter 38, "22 Unforgivable E-mail Mistakes.")

Part Three

What Works

Chapter 26

About the Subject Line

The subject line is as important as anything you put into the body of the e-mail message.

In fact, what we looked at in Chapter 24—that terse, concise template that is easy for people to respond to or forward to someone else—is very likely the least important part of an e-mail message. The most important part of the e-mail message, and the part that I would urge you to pay attention to and strategize more closely than any other part, is the subject line, and that is the subject of our present chapter.

Many people imagine that the subject line of an e-mail is comparatively unimportant, and then wonder why their messages get no response or a confused response. In fact, the subject line of the e-mail is the single most important determinant of whether the person will ever open, read, or acknowledge the body of the message—which means that we need to find a way to strategize that subject line at least as carefully and probably with much more thought than the body of the message.

Here are some examples of subject lines sent by real, live salespeople that are well intentioned enough and are certainly not making any attempt to mislead the reader but that still fail miserably at the task of getting the person to open the message and consider its contents. (I've changed the content of these headings very slightly so as to avoid any confidentiality problems, but trust me, I really have received e-mails with headings like this.)

Subject: Article

Is this a request that I send the person an article? Is this a request that the person be allowed to interview me for an article? Is this a request for an article that I have written? Some people might argue that the ambiguity of the subject line here is a positive, but I have my doubts. Remember, this message is competing against scores or hundreds of other messages for my attention. In fact, the salesperson wanted to send me an article. But if the point was to get me to open the message, the headline, in my view, did a terrible job.

Subject: Your company's success

Again—there's nothing misleading about this. The salesperson really does want to talk to me about my company's success in the body of the e-mail. But what possible entry point to this subject does the single sentence here give me? My company's success depends on any one of a thousand different factors and all I get from a subject heading like this is that the person who's e-mailing me isn't willing to specify which one of those thousands of factors this message relates to.

This is another subject heading that is presumably so vague that it undercuts any actual content of the body of the message that might be of interest to me. In fact, the person was trying to meet with me to discuss ways for me to expand my network of sales training franchises by means of display advertising. I'm not saying he necessarily had to put the words *display advertising* in the heading, but might it have made sense to connect the heading somehow to the goal I already knew about—namely, expanding my franchise network?

Subject: Tomorrow

This is an example of a subject line that is self-contained and has no meaningful connection whatsoever to the message it precedes. Think about it for a second. I can understand two things when I look at the subject line and the heading. I can understand the content of the subject line, in this case "tomorrow," and I can understand whether I recognize who sent the message. If I recognize who the message is coming from, this could be a great heading because I would be interested in finding out what the person has to say about tomorrow. But in this case, I had no idea who this person was, and so I was left a message from a stranger about something unspecified that would happen tomorrow. Would you open that message? The only reason I did was that I was writing this book, and I had a duty to identify what messages hooked up with stupid e-mail headlines. The person who was planning to call "tomorrow" wanted to discuss my investments. I missed the call.

Unless you're writing a book about e-mail techniques and looking for examples of lousy subject headings, as I was, you'll want to find a way to avoid this sort of heading.

So much for well-meaning headlines that fail to engage the recipient. What do the best subject lines look like?

Here is one of my favorites:

Subject: June 23 meeting

The beauty of this heading is that it immediately answers the first question that everybody has when they are considering opening up an e-mail message, namely, "Is this something I really have to look at?"

In this case, the message makes it clear that it is something that requires attention, because there is a meeting in the short term. In fact, when I send this message, what I am doing is asking the person whether he or she is willing to meet with me on a certain date and time. I particularly like placing an emphasis on times and dates and months in headings, because it causes the recipient to wonder whether the message affects his or her immediate schedule. And by immediate schedule, I mean something that takes place during the next two weeks.

Commitments that take place within this particular time frame tend to mean much more than commitments that are made for three months or six months or nine months or twelve months away. The closer we get to that two-week time frame, the more meaningful that commitment is and the more important the communication about it becomes. So it stands to reason that a heading that focuses on a specific date within the next two weeks will probably have more interest than something that does not.

Here is another heading that works:

Subject: Joe Clark

This subject line is a good one to use when Joe Clark is someone known to both the sender and the recipient of the message. If Joe

Clark is a personal acquaintance of the person I am trying to reach out to, it is almost a guarantee that the recipient is going to open the message and see what I have to say about Joe. Obviously I have to follow through on this and mention that Joe gave me a referral or explain how Joe and I have worked together in the past.

Here is another example of an e-mail heading that works:

Subject: McClusky Industries

This is good when McClusky Industries is either a competitor of the e-mail recipient or a company otherwise familiar to the person I am trying to contact. Ideally, it should be a company that I have worked with, so I can build my message around the success I had in working with McClusky in the past.

Chapter 27

The Secret Weapon

How the heck do you carry on an ongoing conversation using that basic template for a good e-mail that you saw in Chapter 24? You can't simply send an endless series of two- or three-sentence e-mails.

For more complex communications as the relationship deepens, it is imperative that you find a way to send a little bit more substantial message and carry on with the business of moving your sales cycle forward. You just have to do this in a way that takes into account two facts about the way people really read e-mail.

Fact Number One: Text is inherently boring, and it's more boring as it accumulates. A huge column of text that has an unbroken series of words and sentences will be almost impenetrable to your reader.

Fact Number Two: Human beings are visually driven organisms. They are driven to graphics. And, in the kind of e-mail messages we're talking about, graphics mean bullet points. Bullet points are your secret weapon.

You know when the personal computer really took off? When somebody invented the visual interface that allowed pictures and icons to replace long lines of text. Apple did it first, then Microsoft shrewdly followed suit with the Windows operating system. Before that, if you were using an IBM-type machine, you were basically looking at columns of text and issuing commands like Control-S, rather than using your mouse to click on a picture. How many gazillion personal computers have Windows today? I don't know, but the number is so huge that Bill Gates has a special section of the IRS all to himself. They need a special suite of computers to keep track of all his assets and the money due to the federal government from those assets. What connected with people? Pictures.

Have you noticed how motion pictures have become the primary art form of our time? What connects with people? Pictures.

Have you noticed how graphic novels have become the most important new literary genre in our era? What connects with people? Pictures.

Have you noticed how PowerPoint, which is visually driven, has emerged as the most important business tool since the word-processing program? Or maybe even since the spreadsheet? What connects with people? Pictures.

There is a reason all these things happened. Human beings respond well to pictures. In other words, we respond more easily and with greater facility to messages that are visual in nature.

I am not going to suggest that you should go out of your way to incorporate lots of snazzy graphics into your e-mail messages. There are some people who would argue that you should do that, but I personally don't think this is a great investment of a salesperson's time, for the simple reason that large graphics files (a) tend to take up a lot of space and (b) are likely to be blocked by spam filters.

No, what I am suggesting is that you keep your messages personal and keep them simple, but that you find ways to incorporate a secret weapon:

Bullet points.

Bullet points serve basically the same purpose as photos or cartoons would in a PowerPoint or other visual demonstration. But they are much easier to incorporate into e-mail messages.

Consider this first draft of an article from sales trainer Marisa Pensa:

Keep your first appointments up . . . whatever it takes. I really don't care if you "cold call," warm call, call only referrals, or call your in-laws and ask them for leads. You can call whoever you want, but you have to call someone, and you have to be absolutely determined about keeping a stream of new business and new appointments flowing at all times. Let me give you some examples of what I mean when I say "whatever it takes." Keep a list with you at all times of names and numbers you can call to set a first appointment. You never know when you'll have from ten minutes to one hour of downtime. Pull out your cell phone and make a few calls. I was recently in Mississippi training, and just starting a five-hour drive home when my engine light came on. My husband insisted that I go have the car checked out before driving home. During my one-hour wait, I was able to make fifteen calls, speak with six decision-makers, and set two appointments—all because I had a list of leads with me! Having this list on my person at all times helps me set roughly 50 percent of my total appointment volume. When I have several days of training back to back, the only way I can keep my appointment total up is to set a goal of pulling out my cell phone and making five calls in the car at the end of the day . . . before my key goes into the ignition. Inevitably, I'll get one or two calls back during my commute home and I will usually set one appointment before I pull into my driveway. Set a lead-generation goal at social events. None of us "really" has time to prospect. All the same, we have to make time. A lead can come from a casual conversation you have with someone at a sporting event, at church, at a family reunion, or from any of a dozen other sources. I set a personal lead-generation goal before almost every large group social event. For instance: I do a series of adventure races every other month, and I always set a goal of two leads per race just by having casual conversation with teammates. I usually finish the race with three to four leads—not two—and get at least one appointment out of each race. Stretch yourself once a quarter by doing a full-day call blitz. See just how many calls you can make in one day. You have to be organized and know who you plan to call *before* the day starts. I do these quarterly and usually average sixty to seventy calls on those days. The real benefit that I gain from these call blitzes (other than setting eight to twelve new appointments in a single day and connecting with many new people) is that it puts my regular goal of five to ten calls per day into perspective. That seems like small potatoes compared to seventy calls in a single day! Make use of personal trips. Why not? My appointments were in bad shape about six months ago and my husband and I had a scheduled vacation coming up in Orlando. I was stressed going into the trip, because my appointments were down. In keeping with the theme of "do whatever it takes," I thought, *Why not go on first appointments while in Orlando?* After all, we were staying at the Orlando World Center Hotel—and they just happen to have a sales team. There was another large company down the street. Before we hit the road, I made three calls and set two appointments based on the fact that I was "going to be in the area." One of those appointments turned into a sale six weeks later. I repeat—do whatever it takes to keep your first appointments up! Failure to do this will, inevitably, have a devastating affect on your morale.

Did you actually read it? I didn't think so. Now, here is the exact same content re-edited so as to incorporate the "bullet principle." It made a powerful impact as part of an e-mail distribution to an "opt-in" list. Take a look:

> Keep your first appointments up . . . whatever it takes.
> *Marisa Pensa mpensa@dei-excel.com*
> I really don't care if you "cold call," warm call, call only referrals, or call your in-laws and ask them for leads. You can call whoever you want, but *you have to call someone,* and you have to be absolutely determined about keeping a stream of new business and new appointments flowing at all times.
> Let me give you some examples of what I mean when I say "whatever it takes":
>
> - Keep a list with you at all times of names and numbers you can call to set a first appointment. You never know when you'll have from ten minutes to one hour of downtime. Pull out your cell phone and make a few calls.
> - I was recently in Mississippi training, and just starting a five-hour drive home when my engine light came on. My husband insisted that I go have the car checked out before driving home. During my one-hour wait, I was able to make fifteen calls, speak with six decision-makers, and set two appointments—all because I had a list of leads with me! Having this list on my person at all times helps me set roughly 50 percent of my total appointment volume.
> - When I have several days of training back to back, the only way I can keep my appointment total up is to set a goal of pulling out my cell phone and making five calls in the car at the end of the day . . . before my key goes into the ignition. Inevitably, I'll get one or two calls back during my commute home and I will usually set one appointment before I pull into my driveway.
> - Set a lead-generation goal at social events. None of us "really" has time to prospect. All the same, we have to make time.
> - A lead can come from a casual conversation you have with

someone at a sporting event, at church, at a family reunion, or from any of a dozen other sources. I set a personal lead-generation goal before almost every large group social event.

- For instance: I do a series of adventure races every other month, and I always set a goal of two leads per race just by having casual conversation with teammates. I usually finish the race with three to four leads—not two—and get at least one appointment out of each race.
- Stretch yourself once a quarter by doing a full-day call blitz. See just how many calls you can make in one day.
- You have to be organized and know whom you plan to call before the day starts. I do these quarterly and usually average sixty to seventy calls on those days.
- The real benefit that I gain from these call blitzes (other than setting eight to twelve new appointments in a single day and connecting with many new people) is that it puts my regular goal of five to ten calls per day into perspective. That seems like small potatoes compared to seventy calls in a single day!
- Make use of personal trips. Why not?
- My appointments were in bad shape about six months ago and my husband and I had a scheduled vacation coming up in Orlando. I was stressed going into the trip, because my appointments were down.
- In keeping with the theme of "do whatever it takes," I thought, "Why not go on first appointments while in Orlando?" After all, we were staying at the Orlando World Center Hotel—and they just happen to have a sales team. There was another large company down the street.
- Before we hit the road, I made three calls and set two appointments based on the fact that I was "going to be in the area." One of those appointments turned into a sale six weeks later.

I repeat—do whatever it takes to keep your first appointments up! Failure to do this will, inevitably, have a devastating affect on your morale.

Of the two versions, which e-mail would you be most likely to scan for good ideas? Which would you be more likely to implement? Which would you be more likely to pass along to someone else?

Here is an example on a much smaller scale, this time involving an e-mail message I might send to a prospect who is considering letting my team make a presentation to a critical group within his organization. Here's the first version.

To: Jim Prospect
From: Mike Salesperson
Subject: Upcoming presentation

Jim:
As you requested, here are some thoughts on why it makes sense for me to deliver the proposal in person in front of your regional vice president on May 3. For one thing, he will get a sense of me as a trainer and see how my personal style connects with the material. For another thing, I will bring twenty-five-plus years of experience to the task of explaining the principles that make up the substance of the program. Finally, I will be able to answer questions on the spot, rather than putting you in the awkward position of having to check with me and follow up afterward about any queries that the vice president may have about the program content. Jim, I really think this is the way to go. What would you think of putting me on the agenda on May 3?

Mike

Now take a look at the same message, reformatted this time using the "bullet principle":

To: Jim Prospect
From: Mike Salesperson
Subject: Upcoming presentation

Jim:
As you requested, here are some thoughts on why it makes sense for me to deliver the proposal in person in front of your regional vice president on May 3. I hope you'll share them with the board.

- For one thing, the RVPs get a sense of me as a trainer and see how my personal style connects with the material.

- For another thing, I will be able to demonstrate the Phone Coach equipment that is a critical part of the training program.
- Finally, I will be able to answer questions on the spot, rather than putting you in the awkward position of having to check with me and follow up afterward about any queries that they may have about the program content.

Jim, I really think this is the way to go. What would you think of putting me on the agenda on May 3?

Mike

Do you see the difference? The same exact information is getting across, but the fact that the information is conveyed by means of bullet points makes the second message much easier to get into. The easier your message is to get into, the more eyeballs will actually read it, and the more eyeballs that actually read it, the more fingers will type a response to you and hit "send."

Chapter 28

Signatures

A major opportunity for spreading the word about your company and its products and services can and should be found at the bottom of every e-mail message you send. This is the portion of the message known as the "signature," and it should be written, revised, and updated as carefully as anything else that appears in your message.

Anyone who must make his or her way through a hundred or so e-mail messages sometimes notices the signature more readily than the body of the message. Why? Because human beings have a tendency to scan to the bottom of a message to see what the point of it is. We want to "cut to the chase"—so we hit that page-down button or use our mouse to scroll to the very bottom of the message. What this means is that someone who receives a number of messages from us will, over time, receive more exposure to the signature we set up at the bottom of the message than to anything else we write!

It behooves us, then, to create a powerful and compelling signature, and to revise it from time to time so it retains the same basic theme but does not become so familiar that its message fades into oblivion.

Just as you would not send out a message to prospects or clients in written form that did not incorporate your company's logo and contact information on a sharp-looking piece of stationery, so you will also want to avoid sending out an e-mail message that contains no reference whatsoever to your company, its Web site, or your own role within the company.

Of course, there are some important differences between a carefully crafted e-mail signature and a good piece of stationery. For one thing, the stationery is a physical object, and it is an accepted convention to incorporate a logo at some point near its upper left-hand corner. There is no such convention these days regarding e-mail signatures, primarily because the act of sending an image as part of a logo can set off spam filter alerts.

Here is a model signature to consider adapting:

Stephan Schiffman, President
D.E.I. Franchise Systems
www.dei-sales.com
"We Understand Sales"
250 W. 57th Street
New York, NY 10107
212-581-7390 (office)
212-555-5557 (cell)
212-555-5556 (home)

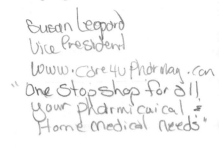

You read right—that's a home phone number. When I leave a positive impression with a prospect or customer, I want it to be reinforced with accurate information on how to reach me by phone at just about any hour of the night or day.

My signature sends the clear and unequivocal commitment that these people can and should feel free to reach out to me at any of the three numbers I offer.

I do get a lot of resistance to this from salespeople, and I have told salespeople in training programs that it is a perfectly acceptable alternative to list one's cell phone number and main office number if these are the only two lines that you want to use for business purposes. But supplying the home number sends a message of accountability that is hard to forget.

Remember this, if you remember anything at all about your e-mail message signatures: It should send the unspoken message that you wish to be accessible to the other person, and it should offer at least two valid phone options that the person can use to get in contact with you.

Chapter 29

The P.S.

When you receive an appeal from the Red Cross or from somebody trying to sell you a new magazine subscription by mail, you virtually always see a P.S. message down at the bottom below the author's signature, whether the document is a single page or longer.

I think the reason that the P.S. message is so powerful in direct mail is that it allows the copywriter to restate all the critical facts of the message and even to issue a call to action. For instance, a P.S. might look like this:

> P.S. Call 1-800-999-9999 today to lock in your special low rate of only $12.95 per unit!

The theory is that the person reading the message may drift down to the P.S. or even zip forward to it and read nothing else but that message.

On the whole I think this is an accurate way to look at direct-mail selling, but notice that in our e-mail message we're not trying to close the deal by means of our message. So if we do use a P.S. to restate key points, we want to make sure that we're not doing so in such a way that's going to make the letter likely to be confused with spam.

Feel free to use a P.S. statement at the end of your message to restate a key point and perhaps emphasize the Next Step you plan to ask for. But make sure that that P.S. is appended to a message that is suitably concise, and be sure you personalize it in such a way that the recipient knows it could only have been addressed to him or her.

Chapter 30

My Pet Peeve

I am devoting an entire chapter to an increasingly common e-mail correspondence habit—because it annoys me. That isn't really such a big deal, but the fact that this habit may be annoying your prospects is a big deal.

What annoys me is messages like this:

Subject: Re: Discussion

Okay, fine. Let's do that.

Did you understand that? Me neither. Nevertheless, I get messages like that from salespeople all the time. They assume I remember what the heck they were talking about. I don't, and neither do your prospects. They open the "conversation" (which I have little or no memory of participating in) with inscrutable phrases like "Why not?" or "Should I ask them first?"

People sometimes lose sight of the fact that the decision-makers with whom they are discussing matters by e-mail have other things going on in their lives. There are multiple priorities, multiple objectives, and multiple contacts to juggle at any given moment. It is therefore incumbent upon you, as a salesperson, to give appropriate context within the body of your message—while keeping the message concise. Offer context that will allow the other person to make sense out of your message even after having had thirty other people interrupt his or her day.

This problem highlights a regrettable disadvantage of e-mail, which is that even though it often *feels* like a conversation to the salesperson, and perhaps even to the person with whom he or she communicating, that "conversation" can be, and often is, interrupted by many other things during the course of the day. So what feels to you, the salesperson, like a small pause may end up feeling to the recipient like a totally different conversation.

Remember, a whole lot can happen between the time you hit "send" at 9:00 in the morning and the time I read your message at 4:00 that afternoon.

Chapter 31

Three Critical E-mail Selling Principles

The principles I want to share with you now are so important that I want to cover each of them here, and offer examples as to what they might look like if they are expressed within the body of an e-mail message. But I also want to make it clear to you that the same principles apply in any setting where you are communicating with a prospect. These principles are relevant to any salesperson, in any industry, anywhere on earth. So whether you're sending e-mail messages, closing sales over the telephone, or casting a large blanket over a campfire in order to send smoke signals from the parking lot, you'll have the opportunity to use these principles to improve your relationship with the prospect (and, simultaneously, the size of the number on your commission check.)

We train a lot of different salespeople in a lot of different industries. Sometimes they put up a fuss and insist that what we're trying to share with them doesn't actually apply to their sale. *That has never, ever happened when we shared the principles you are about to read.*

These three principles, in other words, actually work, *and* they are relevant to any and every selling situation. If you memorize them and use them on a regular basis, you will make more money. That's a promise.

The Three Selling Principles That Are Always Relevant to Every Situation are as follows.

Principle #1. Learn about what they do.
Principle #2. Be more concerned than they are about their problems.
Principle #3. If all else fails, ask where you went wrong or what mistake you made.

Got it? Great. We're done.

Seriously, before you try to implement any of these (deceptively easy-sounding) rules, let me share some insights on *how* to do so, and what kinds of mistakes are likely to present themselves when you incorporate these ideas into your e-mail communications with prospects and customers.

The first of our Selling Principles That Are Always Relevant to Every Situation is:

Learn about what they do.

In selling, we are not so much interested in identifying what the prospective buyer "needs." Instead, we are interested in identifying what he or she is actually doing right now.

Think about it for a second. If I send you an e-mail message asking you to identify your most critical "needs" in XYZ area over the next ten days, what are you going to tell me? You are either going to tell me something superficial and vague about what you are looking for, or you are going to tell me that you do not need anything. That second outcome is considerably more likely. (By the way, if you don't even answer the e-mail message, that's an eloquent way of telling me that you don't think you need anything at all right now.)

Need means "must have." *Need* means "die without." We need water. We need air. We don't need—or at least don't think we need—salespeople to tell us what has to happen next in our business lives.

You will run into a lot of people these days who tell you that sales is all about "finding the need." You will encounter a fair number of experts who insist that effective selling is all about asking "need" or "pain" questions like this:

- "What is it that keeps you up at night?"
- "What is your biggest problem with your current vendor?"
- "What is the one thing you would fix if you could change anything in your relationship with ABC Company?"

Many, many salespeople tell me that messages like this are the focus of their e-mail correspondence campaign with customers and prospects. What's the need? What's the pain?

Here is my question—how much meaningful information are you going to get out of a question like that?

How much meaningful information have you actually received from a question like that?

Instead of focusing on the superficial, need-based, problem-based, pain-based portion of the information picture, I am going to get a better picture of what is actually going on in the relationship if I say something like this:

- "What are you doing right now to . . . ?"
- "How many times before have you . . . ?"
- "Who else have you spoken to about . . . ?"
- "Why did you choose to . . . ?"

Let me give you an example of how this works. Sometimes, if I am in a face-to-face selling situation, I will have the job of determining whether somebody I am talking to is actually the true decision-maker for selecting a sales trainer. No doubt, you have had a similar challenge in face-to-face interviews that you have conducted when *you* are trying to determine whether the person in question really is the decision-maker for what you sell.

So we have a question to ask. What should that question sound like?

Here is what most people ask:

"Are you the final decision-maker for this product?"

Here is what I ask:

"Just out of curiosity, how did you do this the last time?"

Or:

"Just out of curiosity, why did you choose XYZ?"

Or:

"Just out of curiosity, what made you decide to do it X way instead of Y way?"

The responses I get to this will instantly tell me whether the person I am dealing with really is involved in the decision-making process.

Can you see how focusing on the "do" of the situation gives me more information about what is actually happening in that person's world than any other approach?

And you know what? I can ask about the "do" of the situation as it affects this person both *as an employee* and *as an individual.* Two levels! Each informs the other. If I don't know what the other person is trying to "do" professionally—what deadlines are coming up, what new customers have to be kept happy, how old customers are going to be retained—how much progress am I really going to make with this person? And if I don't know what the other person is trying to "do" as an individual in this job—what promotion he or she is after, how he or she got the job, how happy he or she is with the current position—how much progress am I really going to make on the professional front?

If we show genuine, open, and enthusiastic curiosity about what the person is doing on both the personal and organizational level, then we are going to find out that we have a lot higher quality of information and a much more robust picture of what is actually happening in the relationship and in the organization. Certainly we're going to know more if we ask these kinds of questions than we would if we simply fired off a lot of e-mail messages asking the person to tell us what keeps him or her up at night.

If there is nothing that keeps the person up at night, we are in trouble. And even if there is something that keeps the person up at night, we are going to get a better picture of it by asking what they are doing right now to deal with the situation.

We should be curious about the person. We should be curious about the organization.

We should be curious about the past. We should be curious about the present. We should be curious about the future.

We should be curious about how. We should be curious about why.

Wherever possible, build your e-mail messages around a genuine curiosity about what the other person is actually *doing* in an area where you know for sure that you can add value to the person's day.

* * *

The second of our three Selling Principles That Are Always Relevant to Every Situation is:

Be more concerned than they are.

Once you have done an effective job of finding out what the other person is trying to do or accomplish or has done or accomplished in the past, it is incumbent upon you to project yourself into his or her position and express deep, genuine concern about *how* the initiative he or she has committed to—whatever it is—will actually get off the launching pad.

In other words, you want to be *more* upset by the possibility that the contact will not accomplish his or her goal than he or she is.

All too often, people within the target companies we try to sell to have a hard time finding allies to worry or be as concerned as they are about achieving critical goals. In my business, the sales-training business, people are typically trying to increase sales production by a specific percentage marker within a particular period of time. As a sales trainer, I must buy heavily into that goal once I identify it and understand all its parameters. That means I express deep (and quite sincere!) concern about everything connected to that goal—everything that might help my contact attain it, as well as everything that might stand in the way of attaining the goal.

And you know what? When I express a concern about one of those obstacles that might stand in the way of attaining the goal, I will often share a *strategy* for overcoming those obstacles!

So once I have identified what the sales target for the next quarter is—let's say it is exceeding quota by 15 percent in all sales territories—I am going to open up every communication with the people involved and express my concerns about what is standing in the way of our attaining exactly that.

To: Mark Bigshot
From: Stephan Schiffman
Subject: Beating quota by 15 percent in all seventeen of your territories

Mark:

BEATING QUOTA BY 15 PERCENT IN ALL SEVENTEEN OF YOUR TERRITORIES

Great talking to you by phone today. I have some ideas that I think will help you to accomplish this, but I'm concerned about some of the obstacles you're facing. Can we meet in your office this coming Tuesday at 9:00 A.M.?

Stephan Schiffman, President
D.E.I. Franchise Systems
"We Understand Sales"
250 W. 57th Street
New York, NY 10107
212-581-7390 (office)
212-555-5556 (home)
212-555-5557 (cell)

—REQUESTING MEETING AT 9:00 A.M. ON TUESDAY, APRIL 12, 2007—

When I get this meeting (which I will), I am going to mention that I have been very preoccupied with all the possible obstacles standing in the way of Mark's attaining that goal of his. In fact, I am going to enumerate those obstacles in as much detail and with as much emotion as I possibly can. And then I am going to express exactly how much information I have been able to track down that seems relevant to the neutralization of those obstacles, and I am going to talk about the resources that I personally can bring to bear to overcoming them so Mark can attain his goal.

All of this is by way of saying that in your e-mail messages, if you have to pick a single theme that is going to appeal to your prospect, probably one of your best bets will be to select the "message of concern" e-mail. It should look something like the example I've shared with you in this chapter.

* * *

The third of our three Selling Principles That Are Always Relevant to Every Situation is:

If all else fails, ask where you went wrong or what mistake you made.

Assume full responsibility.

What I mean by this is not that you send nonverbal signals of responsibility, or even a formal proclamation to the prospect that you personally are responsible for delivering a positive outcome. Those things are good, of course. But it is just as important to use this principle of taking responsibility to figure out whether you have any daylight, any option to move forward, when things go wrong.

For instance: Suppose you have been working for seven or eight weeks on a major deal, and one morning you receive the voice mail message that salespeople have nightmares about. You hear your primary contact at a huge prospect—one that you thought was at 90 percent likelihood of closing—saying:

"Hi, Jim, this is Bart Overwhelm at Massive Company. I just wanted to let you know we have had a bit of a change of thinking here. I had a chance to chat with the CEO about exactly where we stood on the proposal you put together for us and while I personally think it has all kinds of potential, the CEO feels differently and so we are going to be going a different route. I am sorry this did not work out, but I hope we can keep in touch and possibly get together on another project. Best to you and the kids. Talk to you soon. Bye."

Now suppose that your attempts to reach out to this decision-maker (or purported decision-maker) go nowhere. So you do everything you're supposed to do. You call at 7:00 in the morning. You call at 6:00 at night. You try to get help from Bart's assistant. Nothing works. You cannot get through. You've been shut out.

You have a feeling there *might* be something that could save the deal. If you act fast. But you have no idea what that "something" is.

What to do?

You might be tempted to think that there's nothing you could do wrong at this stage if your goal is to get Bart's attention and re-establish a dialogue. Actually, there is plenty you could do wrong. You could show up in the Massive Company parking lot and howl a lament to the skies. You could hire a skywriting team and a small aircraft to write the words "Surrender, Bart" in the sky above the company's headquarters. But assuming that you are not up for theatrics like those, you will want to focus instead on the one *right* thing to do in this situation, which is what I call the "taking responsibility e-mail."

It could look like this:

Subject: My CEO

. . . wants to know what I did wrong here. I feel like I must have screwed something up. Did I miss something?

Jim Jarhead
WidgetCo

Want to hear about an even more effective message? This would be for your boss or CEO to send the message. (Hey, you're not proud. If it would help you land a huge deal, now or in the future, would it be worth asking your CEO to send an e-mail message? Sure it would.)

Here is how it might look. Remember, this is coming from the CEO's e-mail address.

Subject: Jim Jarhead

Just between you and me—what did Jim do wrong on that proposal?

Ed Intensely
CEO
WidgetCo
212-555-5555

Messages like these have an extraordinary galvanizing effect. (Another strategy that is just as powerful is for your CEO to make a call, leaving a message "Concerning Jim Jarhead"—with no other information besides his title and contact number—on your contact's voice mail.)

In almost all situations, the person you are reaching out to will in fact respond, and fast, with an explanation of what happened. You might not get the deal, but you will get the straight story about what actually caused you to fall out of the running so suddenly. The response, whether it comes by e-mail, voice mail, or somebody actually picking up the phone when you call, is probably going to sound like this:

"Actually, Jim did not do anything wrong at all. It's just us. We found out that our budgets are frozen for the next six months and we do not have any way to pay for this. I wish I had known that up front, because I certainly would have told Jim that was the situation so that he could have avoided putting all this effort and time into setting up the proposal. But that is where we stand."

At this point, it might be a good idea for your CEO—or whoever—to suggest billing the program or product delivery later, to take advantage of the budget allocation that will unfold.

When in doubt, use e-mail to take responsibility. When something goes wrong, ask where you went wrong or what mistake you made. Then try to get face to face, or at least voice to voice, so someone in your organization can offer a suggestion about how to get around the problem that's presented itself.

Chapter 32

E-mail "Branding"

We have entered a fascinating period in human history, one in which a single piece of information can emerge as a defining identifier and even a determinant of your own identity.

Think about it. If you have an e-mail address that connects to your business—*Johnsmith@ABCcorp.com*—then, when you share that information with someone, you are not merely giving them a way of getting in touch with you but are also sharing an important piece of who you are.

By giving the person that e-mail address, you give him or her the right to begin a correspondence with you, to maintain that correspondence over time, to forward it to other people, and to reach out to you at any and every time the person feels it's appropriate to do so—2:00 in the morning, 1:00 in the afternoon, whatever. In a strange way, your business persona *melds* with that e-mail address, in a way that your business identity does not meld with a phone number or a physical address. In cyberspace, your e-mail address is not only a way to get in touch with you but also an expression of your business self.

The reason I bring this up is to remind you that when you share your e-mail address with a business contact, you are basically sharing the right to archive and retrieve an ongoing series of messages that you share. E-mail is different from written correspondence in that it tends to stick around for a while. Whereas we can throw away a written memo, it is quite common for electronic correspondence records to exist in three or four or more forms. This is not to suggest that you should become paranoid about giving out your e-mail address—quite the contrary; you should relish the opportunity to create and support a "business identity" that sends a consistent brand message about you and the organization you represent.

Just as your company goes out of its way to send specific brand messages about its products and services, you can and should use your e-mail address to evoke certain distinctive brand messages about you as a person: your trustworthiness, for instance, and your ability to respond quickly to questions, your diligence in following through on commitments, and so forth. Just make sure the messages you send are consistently positive ones, and you will have no problem.

And—to support your brand—do be sure to check your e-mail at least once a day. (Any other standard is tantamount to sales malpractice these days.)

Chapter 33

E-mail and Online Newsletters

Just about everyone on earth who has an e-mail account hates spam.

By the same token, just about everybody on earth likes to get something valuable for free. Someone may ask to receive something you or your business offer for free—an article or a report, say. The act of your signing prospects up for an e-mail newsletter is not spam, assuming that you give them the option to remove themselves from the distribution list, and assuming that you honor their request if they make it.

We must learn to operate between two all-too-familiar extremes—flooding somebody with irrelevant, unsolicited information on the one hand, and giving away "too much" free content online. Ultimately, of course, it's a matter of trial and error, but this is a balancing act that you and your company can, with just a little practice, get right.

People who agree to have their e-mail addresses added to a distribution list usually receive what is known as an "opt-in" newsletter. There's a pretty obvious reason for this name: they have opted in to the distribution list, meaning they have agreed to receive your newsletter.

At my company, DEI Franchise Systems, we have a free booklet on starting your own franchise business that anyone who visits our Web site can request. The act of making the request for the free booklet—which we send along to anybody who requests it—enrolls you on our e-mail distribution list. We have also purchased opt-in e-mails from e-mail list brokers. Between the two sources, we have compiled a master list with the names of approximately 13,000 people who have requested our content. Every single one of those names belongs to somebody who once agreed to give their e-mail address in exchange for receiving something in return. And every single one of them can opt out as easily as they opted in.

Our challenge, in working with this list, is to make absolutely certain that we are having a good dialogue with these people and that they feel that the information they receive as a result of joining the list is worthwhile.

So what do I send them? Well, approximately once a week, I send out an article—and a request for information. I want to know what kind of topics they would like to see covered in future newsletters. I may also use the list to broadcast information about upcoming public events that involve DEI or my own speaking appearances.

Obviously, I am hoping to encourage a dialogue by means of passing along specific helpful information to this group, which consists almost exclusively of salespeople, sales managers, and senior executives at companies. Some of those conversations turn into discussions about face-to-face training programs. And some of those discussions, thank goodness, actually turn into revenue for me and my company. The key to getting a good dialogue going, in my experience, is picking content that seems likely to be easy to implement for the people in my opt-in list.

I mentioned a little bit earlier that the e-mail newsletter to this opt-in list goes out "approximately" once a week. That is a conscious decision. One of the mistakes that people make about e-mail newsletters is that they make them too predictable.

If the newsletter always comes out on Monday or always comes out on the first of the month, people become attuned to it—and that can be a bad thing. It's possible, of course, that the person is eagerly awaiting the latest installment of the e-newsletter, just waiting for the moment he or she can read the articles and forward them to everybody else in the organization. To my way of thinking, though, the odds are fairly long against that possibility. Much more likely is the scenario where the person gets habituated to seeing the newsletter show up in the mailbox on a certain day and learns to ignore it.

So by altering the production schedule—by making it come out on the tenth day and then on the fourth day and then on the ninth day and then on the eleventh day—we help the audience develop a sense that the content is on the way at some point in the future. But we do not set up a pattern that they become so used to that they instantly delete the newsletter every Monday morning.

Along the same lines, I try to alter the headings that I use in setting up the subject line for my e-mail newsletter. Here are some examples of actual headings that we have used with the newsletter. Notice that each and every one is different.

Subject: Stephan Schiffman on increasing the value of your key accounts
Subject: Ten "musts" for a successful speech
Subject: Sixty-second overview: Time management techniques for salespeople
Subject: DEI Update: The five stages of the sales career
Subject: Sales managers: Are you measuring these fifteen skills?

Here's what I *don't* do for the subject line:

Subject: Stephan Schiffman's E-Newsletter, Volume 2, Issue 4

It never ceases to amaze me. People really do repeat subject lines like that for their newsletters, week after week after week. No benefit, no highlight—just the name of the newsletter and the volume and issue number. How boring is that?

Vary your subject lines. Vary your content. And always highlight the benefit the person will receive by clicking on your message.

Chapter 34

On Opt-In Lists

Here are some thoughts on creating and managing your opt-in lists.

Failing to give people an opportunity to give you their e-mail address is a big mistake. If you have a Web site, you should have a place there where people can get something free—if only your company's brochure in PDF format—in exchange for giving you their e-mail address. You will need to develop a form that makes it easy for people to give you this information. Free resources on how to build such a form can be found at *www.htmlgoodies.com/tutorials/forms/index.php*.

Do not ignore requests from people who want to be taken off your list. We use a tool called EmailLabs, which I recommend highly—you can find out more about it at *www.emaillabs.com*.

One of the things I like about EmailLabs is that it makes it extremely easy to manage drop requests. There is a single spot where you can pop in a given e-mail address, as the software will instantly ensure that the e-mail address in question is utterly and completely deleted from any and all distribution lists that you may be managing. In other words, if you have fifteen or so distribution lists that you are keeping track of—and we do at my company—EmailLabs gives you a single step you can take to make absolutely sure that a drop request has been honored by each and every one of those fifteen lists.

Create messages that look cool. Another thing that I like about EmailLabs is that it gives you an extremely easy interface for HTML code development. To put this in the language of the layman (which I certainly am), their "HTML helper" feature allows people who only know how to use a program like Microsoft Word to create an extremely attractive newsletter—without having to master HTML programming skills.

Here's an example of a recent newsletter we created:

Stephan Schiffman's
Six Ways to Improve Major Account Penetration

(New York, NY, March 30, 2006)—Not long ago, a client of ours in the telecommunications industry asked us to help set up a customized training program to help sales representatives increase market share within its own major accounts.

This particular client had numerous *Fortune* 100 customers—but had not yet developed a systemized way of identifying new areas for growth within each of these accounts.

We asked all the participants to bring information on their top five accounts to our training session. At the program, we asked them to answer the following six questions (and their follow-ups) about each account:

1. How can I work with this company's sales department to win new customers—and increase profitability? *Follow-up questions:* What new people within the organization would I have to talk to about new customer development? Who could point me toward those people?

2. How can I help the target company's sales, customer service, shipping, and transportation departments to maintain its base of existing accounts more effectively? *Follow-up questions:* What new people within the organization would I talk to about maintaining existing accounts? Who could point me toward those people?

3. How can I work with the target company's shipping, accounts receivable, accounts payable, and manufacturing departments to improve communications with major suppliers? *Follow-up questions:* What new people within the organization would I talk to about improving communications with suppliers? Who could point me toward those people?

4. What programs can I put together with this company's marketing and sales departments to help the organization gain a competitive edge in the marketplace? *Follow-up questions:* What new people within the organization would I talk to about improving the company's competitive position? Who could point me toward those people?

5. How can I help this company's department heads and human resources people retain and recruit high-quality employees? *Follow-up questions:* What new people within the organization would I talk to about human resource issues? Who could point me toward those people?
6. What can I propose to this company's shipping, receiving, dispatching, sales, and customer service people to help streamline transportation and operations? *Follow-up questions:* What new people within the organization would I talk to about streamlining transportation activities? Who could point me toward those people?

We asked the salespeople to identify specific contacts in each of these different areas for all five of the person's "top accounts."

The salespeople also wrote down the size of each account, what had already been sold there, the possible product application by division or department, and a summary of the information that they either already had, or could get easily.

At this point, all the participants had a huge number of new opportunities to exploit. We then prioritized their new to-do list according to four criteria:

- Territory management considerations (i.e., which contacts to meet with in the same building on a given day)
- Potential account size
- Likely time cycle
- Whether the group or person we were reaching out to had actually been helped in the past by this telecom company

Based on these four criteria, we set up a battle plan for the next thirty days for each representative. Dramatic income growth within the major account base followed!

By asking these same six questions, and their follow-ups, your team can set up the same kind of thirty-day battle plan, one that targets—and wins— more and bigger deals within your company's major account base.

STEPHAN SCHIFFMAN is the president of D.E.I., one of the largest sales training companies in the U.S. He is the author of a number of best-selling books including *Cold Calling Techniques (That Really Work!)*, and *The 25 Sales Habits of Highly Effective Salespeople*, and *Stephan Schiffman's Telesales*. Schiffman's writings have appeared in many publications, including *The Wall Street Journal*, *The New York Times*, and *INC.* magazine. For more information about Schiffman and D.E.I. Management, please call (800) 224-2140 or visit *www .dei-sales.com.*

Don't waste time sending messages to bad e-mail addresses. Yet another thing I like about EmailLabs is its ability to handle and eliminate "bounce backs"—those pesky messages that come your way when an address is invalid for some reason or out of date. Get them out of your list quickly.

Learn how to manage exclusion lists. Just as there are some people who do not want to receive e-mail from you, there are also some people you may not want to be sending e-mail to yourself. Did you realize that your competitors have access to your Web site? Well, they do, and it is a pretty good bet that they are using your stuff if you are circulating a free e-mail newsletter. If you do not want somebody who is directly or indirectly competing with you to have access to all the material you are putting together, you can enter the appropriate domain names into a suppression list. Again, EmailLabs is excellent in this regard, as it has a suppression feature that is extremely easy to use.

Back up everything. What you want to avoid is having any situation where a catastrophic accident or unforeseen computer glitch instantly vaporizes twenty or thirty thousand contact names at a time. If you are handling this information on your own, you will want to make sure you back up everything (as in weekly or monthly) by transferring your database into a format comprehensible to a database program or spreadsheet. Keep a separate file accessible at all times.

You may be tempted to assume from the previous that I have been lavishly compensated by the good people at EmailLabs in exchange for the complimentary things that I have said about them in this part of the book. That is not true. What you have read here is based solely on my own experience with the software, and with the good results that it has delivered for us. It is, I can say without reservation, an excellent product: easy to use, reliable, and regularly updated. There are other resources available out there that you can use to manage and create your opt-in e-newsletter campaign, but I think I have given you a pretty clear indication here about which one I think you should be using.

Chapter 35

E-mail and Article Distribution

I love using e-mail to alert prospects and customers to the fact that an article about my company has shown up in a media source unconnected with my company. At the end of these messages, I usually suggest that the prospect and I get together to discuss new ideas. (But notice that the e-mail is technically "about" the link I'm passing along.)

Sometimes, when I suggest that salespeople use e-mail for just this purpose, they balk at the idea, and say, more or less, the following:

"That's all very well for you, Steve—you're an author with lots of experience in getting articles placed. How the heck am I supposed to point people toward articles about my company when none exist?"

Well, I have two responses. First of all, how sure are you that articles about you, your company, or your products really don't exist? Have you entered your own name or your company's name or the name of your most popular products and services into Google, the omnipresent search engine of our time? Once you do this simple experiment—and we're talking about an experiment that takes only five to ten minutes to perform—my prediction is that you will find more than one article that's easy for you to pass along to prospects and customers by means of a message like the following.

Subject: Warranty coverage article you might find interesting

Hi Todd:

Below is a link for an article I came across in the Yahoo! News section the other day. It had some interesting points about our recent product launch, and I thought you might find particularly interesting the piece at the end about choosing the right warranty coverage.

  http://linkarticle.com/87890708970

I have some ideas for Q4 I'd like to share with you over lunch next week. I'll call tomorrow to see when you're free.

Take care,
Susan

Now, on to the second point. Even if you do have some coverage of your company, your products, or even yourself that you feel like sharing with the world of prospects and customers, it's likely that you could use more. Believe it or not, it's not at all difficult to put together a strong article that delivers value to your prospective customers—see Chapter 33 on e-mail newsletters and Chapter 36 on blogs—and it's only a very small investment of time, effort, cash, and energy to place those same articles in venues where they'll get more visibility than they're getting right now. Check out the following sites for more information on how to get more exposure for the articles you've developed:

www.prnewswire.com
www.marketwire.com

You can also make this sending-a-link message a "staying in touch" e-mail—one that doesn't (directly) reference a Next Step, but simply gives you a reason to call the person a day or so after you hit "send." Here's how it works. First, you pick someone you want to reconnect with—say, that prospect who's been "pending" for the last three weeks and hasn't gotten back in touch with you about your proposal. Next, you select an article with diligent care, making sure that it really does match something that is happening in this person's world. Then, you place the easiest call in the world: "Hey, I sent you an article on yada yada yada; I don't know if you had the chance to see it, but I wanted to let you know that it's on your e-mail system. How are things?"

I wasn't calling you about trying to get business.

I wasn't even calling to check whether the person remembered the last e-mail message I sent. (That's a no-no—see Chapters 12 and 13.)

I was calling to *make sure he didn't miss* the article about yada yada yada—it's on his e-mail system. "And listen, as long as I've got you on the line . . . what's up in your world?"

I much prefer making this type of call to somebody I would like to work with than any other kind of call. I *hate* (and will not make) the call where I say, "Hey, you told me you were going to have a decision about working with us this week, and it's already Friday. What the heck is the deal?"

Talk about a call that isn't going anywhere! Why bother? You remember what we learned about controlling the flow and people responding in kind? That's not the flow I want. That's not the response that I want to hear back in kind.

So I don't call to ask, "What the heck is holding us up?" Ever. If I have some other reason to initiate contact—the article on yada yada—then in nine instances out of ten the person will, on his or her own, bring up the issue that I really want to talk about—namely, the thing that's standing in the way of us doing business together. Then I can suggest a Next Step that makes sense for both of us.

Chapter 36

E-mail and Blogging

For those of you who have been under a rock for the past few years, a "blog" is simply a diary or journal that somebody shares with the rest of the world via the World Wide Web. The term comes from the phrase "Weblog," and the fact that that six-letter word—shortening the phrase World Wide Web Log—has been further condensed to the monosyllabic "blog" is as telling a signal as I can think of that our world's attention span is collapsing.

Now we don't even have time to say "Weblog." We only have time to say "blog."

Most people who write blogs write them for very small audiences—and by very small audiences I specifically include audiences that do not exceed one. That's the bad news about blogging. What is the good news about blogging? The good news is it is, technically, free. In other words, assuming you have access to the Internet and a fairly reliable connection that gives you access to a Web resource for your blog, actually composing the entries on the journal will be as free as the air you and I breathe—or at least part of the monthly package you are paying for anyway to connect to the Internet.

The six-million-dollar question is this: Why should anyone be interested in reading your blog? Well, there are two possible reasons for people to be interested. Either what you write will entertain them, or what you write will be useful to them.

Let's tackle entertainment first. Many, many people spend large amount of time, effort, and energy trying to be controversial, funny, or otherwise engaging by means of a blog these days, and very few of them succeed. Of those who do succeed, only a tiny minority attract any audience of any size. The question here is not whether you are capable of writing something that makes *you* feel good for having written it, but whether you can write something that will enhance the visibility—and perhaps even the profitability—of your products and services. So I am going to suggest that you focus not on tickling people's funny bones—or, God forbid, infuriating people by being purposely controversial or abusive—but rather on being useful. The job of your blog should be to keep people abreast of new developments that they are likely to be interested in, given their status as your customers or prospects. Leave the entertainment to the pros.

Yes. I am asking you to think of your online journal (if you decide to keep one) as something that people familiar with your stuff, or searching for something like it on the Internet, will be happy to stumble across. I am also suggesting that you merge your e-mail newsletter content with your blog content, and find ways through both channels to share roughly the same information about what it is your company is actually doing these days. Use your blog to:

- Tell people about changes in your product or service lines.
- Tell people about changes to your Web site.
- Share free advice that people can use instantly on how to do what they do better.
- Share links to articles of interest to people who fall into your market niche.
- Collect responses and feedback from blog readers.
- Update your readers about a business or news event that connects to their business objectives.

Of course, each and every one of these ideas is something you could also adapt to your e-mail newsletter copy.

So how do you do it? How do you set up a blog? There are really two options. The first is to purchase software, and the second is to use an online source to power your blog. Two of the most popular are blogger. com and livejournal.com. Check them both out: I think you will decide that working with one of these two sites makes the most sense.

A side note—don't bother trying to promote your business by participating in newsgroups. If you want to join a newsgroup, do so because you enjoy communicating about its subject. Don't assume that the newsgroup will produce prospects in any predictable way.

If you want, and if the editors of the group agree, you can include your name and contact information in the signature of your posting software and share an occasional article or resource or comment. As I say, though, you shouldn't expect this to turn into a revenue source.

Chapter 37

E-mail as a C-Level
Selling Tool

Suppose you follow the advice of the various "take it to the top" C-level selling experts, muster your courage, and actually make that dreaded call to Jane Intimidator, the CEO of Amalgamated Data.

Please understand: At this stage I am not talking about sending a "blind" e-mail message to Jane. I am talking about calling her up on the phone and asking her for a meeting.

And suppose that Jane is actually willing to meet with you. Suppose that she actually remembers and is present for your meeting when you show up at her doorstep.

How long do you think that discussion with Jane is actually going to last?

If Jane is like most of the CEOs that I deal with, it's going to be a pretty brief conversation. Why is it going to be brief? Because Jane got to be CEO of Amalgamated Data by delegating work to other people. So whatever it is I am trying to sell Jane—sales training, computers, sewing machines, rubber mats for the floors of her factory in Thailand, or the little paper umbrellas you put in tropical drinks at the company's annual retreat in Maui—you can bet that Jane is not going to sweat out the details of the decision to implement it. Even if Jane likes my suggestion (and eventually signs on), somebody else is going to do the heavy lifting.

No, the best outcome I can hope for in that situation, and in any similar situation with a similarly high-powered executive, is to receive an endorsement from Jane that allows me not just to *talk* with Joe Achiever, the high-flying VP of Operations for Amalgamated Data, but to do so *under the auspices* of the CEO, Jane Intimidator.

Do you see where I am going with this yet?

Before I leave my meeting with Jane, I want to ensure that I can keep her in the loop—and broadcast the message to others at

Amalgamated Data that Jane is engaged with me and supports my efforts. I want Jane to be kept up to date on exactly what happens between me and Joe, and I want that to happen in a way Joe has to respect.

It might be nice if Jane would agree to meet with me again so I can update her on exactly what is happening between me and Joe. But in the real world, this is not very likely.

No, what is actually likely to happen is that Jane will agree, if I ask her directly, to let me update her on all the important conclusions that Joe and I reach *after* Jane refers me to him.

How do I want to make those updates to Jane? Well, if I know how Jane likes to communicate, I am going to pick the medium she is most likely to engage with, review regularly, and trust. But in a lot of these situations, I really will not have any idea what Jane's preferred method of communication is going to be, so I am going to suggest, by default, that I keep Jane—and everybody else I connect with at Amalgamated Data—up to date by means of e-mail messages. That's why I'm going to ask Jane to give me her e-mail address, so I can personally give her a summary, from time to time (not every day), of exactly what I am doing with Joe. And I can copy Joe on the very same message.

It is very important to understand that when I ask Jane for her e-mail address so I can give her *occasional* updates, what I am really doing is setting up a barometer of sorts that will tell me about the quality of my communication with Jane. I want to gauge Jane's willingness to get an occasional summary of how my initiative is going, and the prospects that it really will add value to her organization.

If Jane tells me, "No, I don't want to give you my e-mail address. I get enough messages already . . . work with purchasing," that is really not a good sign that I should invest a lot of time and effort and energy in my discussions at Amalgamated. It is possible, of course, that Jane would rather hear about how my discussions with Joe are going by some other medium, but if the simple request for an e-mail address—which is, after all, a pretty common means of keeping in touch with the business world these days—falls flat, then I know that there is likely to be a problem somewhere down the line.

In that situation, to identify where I really stand, I might even consider asking Jane a question like this: "Wow. I'm a little surprised by that. I didn't expect that you'd say that. Usually at this stage of a conversation, when I've talked to some of your colleagues at other companies in your industry, they're more than happy to have me set up these updates by e-mail. I'm just curious, why wouldn't you want to get an update from me about how well or poorly things are going?"

By asking this question, I am actually very likely to get a direct answer from the CEO, one that might sound like this: "No, it's nothing like that, Steve. It's just that we're really not planning on doing any spending in this area over the next twelve months. You're probably better off trying to talk to somebody else."

My experience is that CEOs tend to be very direct about things like this. If they are asked a direct question, they will give you, more often than not, a direct answer. That really is the key: You have to be willing to ask them a direct question. You have to learn not to beat around the bush.

Another big issue in this situation is trust. We have to make it absolutely clear to Jane that we will not be bombarding her with fifty e-mails a day. Who could blame her for wanting to avoid that? So we have to make it abundantly clear, from the very beginning of the conversation, that what we are talking about is an e-mail that will take place at some point between Time Frame A and Time Frame B, say fourteen to twenty-one days from now.

You remember that earlier on I told you that sales was all about getting commitment to a Next Step. In this case, when you are dealing with a very high-level person, you may not be able to secure a Next Step that takes the form of a face-to-face meeting with the very topmost person in the organization. (No matter what anybody says, it is unlikely that you will be able to work directly with the CEO of a large organization, and it is unlikely that he or she will agree to meet again with you one on one.)

The whole point of the meeting, from the CEO's point of view, will simply be to plug you in with the right people in the organization. That's if you're lucky. That's the best possible outcome to that meeting. In that case, you will want to "take the temperature" of the relationship and just make sure that the CEO really does want results of the kind you think you can deliver. If so, he or she should have no problem agreeing to a *brief* e-mail message from you that summarizes how the initiative is going.

Once you establish that, the e-mail message you prepare for the CEO will have the most remarkable effect on others in the organization. It will remind Joe Achiever that you are in fact working with Jane Intimidator's blessing. During your next discussion with Joe, you can make it clear that you set up this arrangement with Jane, that she has given you her e-mail address, and that she wants to have a concise summary of exactly what you found out between now and the middle of March.

Let me be honest about something. You cannot expect to play this card alone to victory, because obviously Joe has a relationship with Jane Intimidator, too, and in all likelihood, it is significantly stronger than yours is. But you can make it clear that you are each working along the same lines, in the same direction, and toward the same goals. You can make it clear that implementing Jane's vision is the whole reason you are showing up to meet with Joe. If you use e-mail to send and reinforce that message, you'll be on the right track.

Part Four

What Not to Do

Chapter 38

22 Unforgivable E-mail Mistakes

There are any number of mistakes salespeople make in composing e-mail messages. In this part of the book, I'm going to warn you about twenty-two of the most dangerous—and offer some advice on what to do instead.

Mistake #1: Not Asking for, Confirming, or Setting a Next Step
Not building a reference to some kind of Next Step into your e-mail, or preparing for one you plan to ask for, means breaking a basic commandment of selling.

You are a salesperson. Your income is built on asking for, and receiving, Next Steps. You are communicating by e-mail with someone to whom you wish to sell. It follows that your every communication should propose, or directly or indirectly reference, what's happening next or could happen next in the relationship.

Use a personalized e-mail message to:

- Request a face-to-face meeting at a specific date and time.
- Confirm a face-to-face meeting at a specific date and time.
- Send along a link to an article of interest, then phone the person afterward to make sure the person saw the link. (As I've mentioned elsewhere in this book, I like to do this with people who are "still thinking" about a proposal, and it has been pending for a while. Inevitably, they volunteer information about where they are in the selling process, at which point I can recommend, over the phone, appropriate Next Step.)
- Say that you have a new idea to discuss and suggest a specific date and time for doing so. (This is often helpful after a presentation has gone poorly).

- Set expectations for an upcoming meeting at a specific date and time.
- Establish timelines with a current customer.
- Float an idea for a proposal before you actually deliver the formal proposal at a specific date and time.
- Pave the way for a phone call at a specific date and time that will set up a face-to-face meeting.
- Confirm the date and time of a post-meeting "debriefing" appointment before you deliver a presentation to a committee or meet with a group.

Personally, I don't like "confirming" an initial face-to-face meeting I've recently set up, since that gives the recipient an opportunity to cancel the meeting. If you've already established a good initial dialogue with the person, however, you may wish to confirm the meeting by e-mail or phone contact ahead of time.)

Mistake #2: Stupid Subject Lines

The following messages are very likely to be instantly discarded or ignored. Don't use them.

- Messages whose subject line pretends that the person has already won something
- Subject lines that reference nonexistent acquaintances
- Subject lines that use off-color jokes (or outright obscenity)
- Subject lines featuring any variation on "What on earth do I have to do to get in touch with you?"
- Subject lines featuring any variation on "You asked me to get in touch with you" when that is not the case
- Lies (for instance, "We found your wallet")
- Half-truths (for instance, "We might have found your wallet")

Would *you* open any of those messages? I didn't think so.

Mistake #3: Tone Mismatch

I'm assuming you were careful enough to send an *initial* message that struck a professional tone and piqued the other person's interest.

What I'm talking about here is the message you send *in response to an incoming message from the other person.* Often, the messages sales-people send out in such situations are hastily composed, and they miss out on important conversational cues from the other side.

Put bluntly: We're sometimes so excited about getting a response that we write text that looks as though it were composed by baboons.

Suppose you get the following message:

To: Jerry Salesperson
From: Mark Bigshot
Subject: Re: Beating quota by 15 percent in all seventeen of your
territories

Hello there, Jerry:
This does sound intriguing. Alas, I'm not available to meet with you on April 12.

Is there any time the following week that we could get together? I am free from 2:00 to 3:00 P.M., Monday through Thursday. What's the best day for you?

Best,
Mark

What can we conclude about the person's communication style, just from those few sentences? Well, for one thing, we can conclude that this is someone who takes a good deal of time to compose text with care. All the capitalization is correct. All the punctuation is cor-rect. All the sentences are complete. Mark even used the word *Alas,* which is at least circumstantial evidence of an English major some-where in his family tree.

Since we know that we're dealing with a careful writer who adopts a studious, careful, almost academic tone, we should do our best to mirror that tone in the message we send back. All too often, however, we don't do that. Instead, we tell ourselves that the most important thing is to get back to Mark *instantly.* Nothing else matters! We may even fool ourselves into believing that Mark is probably sitting at his monitor, waiting impatiently for our response, at this very moment. So what do we do? We send something like this:

To: Mark Bigshot
From: Jerry Salesperson
Subject: Re: Beating quota by 15 percent in all seventeen of your territories

hey Mark:
what abt next Mon at 1:30?
I"ll be mtg w/another client that AM near you pls advise
J

Even though we will have to take a few extra minutes to compose a sentence or two that matches Mark's studious tone, we are better advised to do that than to hit "Send" upon composing the barely comprehensible message here. The following is a better model:

To: Mark Bigshot
From: Jerry Salesperson
Subject: Re: Beating quota by 15 percent in all seventeen of your territories

And hello to you, Mark:
Thanks so much for getting back to me so quickly.
    Could we possibly meet in your offices on Monday, the 19th of April, at 1:30? I have a meeting that morning at Centennial Bank.
    Looking forward to hearing from you,

Jerry

A side note: Unless you are absolutely certain you have achieved what might be called a "verbal" level of e-mail interaction with your correspondent—the kind of relationship in which an occasional misspelled word or forgotten punctuation mark will do you no discredit—you really should go to the trouble of composing your message carefully, checking it for grammar and spelling errors, and perhaps even asking somebody else to review it before you send it out. Hitting send before you are really ready to is one of the most common causes of "e-mail stress" among salespeople. By the way, most good e-mail platforms now feature a spell check function, but be forewarned that this function will not correct misspellings of proper names or errors like "lead" for "led." I once lost a prospect after thoroughly confusing him by making a reference to "gold" when I was actually asking about "golf." That is the kind of thing that slips through spell checks, and it something you should be vigilant about, especially when suggesting a round of golf to a high-ranking C-level decision-maker.

Mistake #4: Getting the Person's Name, Company, or Title Wrong

Unforgivable. Check the person's name, company affiliation, and title against an unimpeachable outside source. Again, it is quite possible for you to get the person's name, company, or title wrong . . . and for such a message to sneak past a computerized spell check program. If the person disengages from your message for a heartbeat, that heartbeat is long enough for him or her to hit "delete."

Mistake #5: Sending Attachments Too Early in the Relationship

Sometimes spam filters will refuse a message that carries an attachment, or they will regard an image within the message as an attachment. Even if the message with an attachment or image makes it through, people will generally shy away from a message from an unfamiliar correspondent that has an attachment. Can we blame them? This is how computer viruses are spread. Leave off the attachment until the other person tells you that it is okay to send one.

It is worth noting here that there has been a constant battle between people engaged in sending out voluminous amounts of e-mail unsolicited and the forces of technology committed to keeping people from having to deal with vast amounts of spam. This battle is an ongoing one, in which one side perpetually attempts to top the most recent technological work-arounds and insights of the other. I am going to strongly suggest that you keep your messages *very simple*, lest you be perceived as one of the bad guys. I am also going to suggest that you avoid wasting your time and energy trying to figure out ways to get around spam filters and firewalls. If you are having difficulty connecting with an individual by means of e-mail, pick up the phone and try calling the person directly. That will be a much better investment of your time and effort than convening a summit conference of engineers and asking them to close the gap between you and the prospective customer's IT department.

Mistake #6: Sending the Wrong Attachment

This can be particularly embarrassing if you send an attachment that is non-work-related or contains sensitive information.

Mistake #7: Sending No Attachment When the Body of Your Message References an Attachment

I have a theory that salespeople are the members of the work force most likely to commit this blunder. It is a great way to extend your selling cycle and confuse your prospect. Check twice before you hit "send."

Mistake #8: Using All Caps

This is the online equivalent of shouting at someone across a desk.

They say President Clinton had a habit of sending e-mail messages with the "caps lock" key on. That's just one of the examples by which his presidency is destined to live in infamy. (Capital letters in subject lines are okay in certain situations where your aim is to signal emphasis.)

Mistake # 9: Cursing or Using Off-Color Humor

No bad words. No innuendo. No Monica jokes (see above).

Mistake #10: Using Humor That Is Not Off-Color, But Is Nevertheless Inappropriate

Ethnic jokes, for instance, are off-limits.

Humor in general is an iffy proposition in e-mail correspondence. Much of the interpersonal connection that makes a joke funny in the first place is missing online, thanks to the absence of body language and vocal inflection. (No, little smiley faces are not appropriate in sales communications.) And let's face it—people have gotten tired of having the same joke forwarded to them by fifty different people.

Even well-intentioned humor can backfire in an e-mail message to a prospect or customer. My basic rule is: Save the jokes for the New Year's Eve party, choose them carefully, and tell them in person.

Mistake #11: One-Word Messages

Even in response to a one-word message from the other person and even if the person does understand you (which is far from a certain thing), you will run the risk of being perceived as arrogant. Do something a little more creative than writing "yes" or "no" in the body of the message.

Mistake #12: Ranting

Don't ever send an e-mail message to a prospect or customer when angry. Don't ever send an e-mail message to a prospect or customer in order to "get something off your chest."

Mistake #13: Making Any Reference to Religion

There is only one possible exception to this: The prospect brings the topic of religion up first, and you and the prospect or customer are of the same faith. In this case, you have a possible opportunity for establishing commonality—but this type of discussion is still fraught with risk. Tread carefully. Remember, you are selling, not preaching.

Mistake #14: Making Sexist or Racist Remarks, Even in Jest

Any discriminatory language may come back to haunt you. Always assume the person with whom you're speaking has no sense of humor. Always assume that your message will be archived and/or sent to your boss.

Mistake #15: Communicating in Long Blocks of Text

Break it up and use bullet points, as discussed in Chapter 27.

Mistake #16: Using Cheesy Tricks in Your Subject Line to Try to Get Past the Person's Spam Filter

By using the number 3 instead of an *e*, for example, as in: LOW INT3R3ST RAT3S. Why on earth would you resort to this trick if you weren't sending massive amounts of blind e-mail?

There is probably no better way to convince your correspondent that you are in fact a spam artist.

Mistake #17: Sending the Message to People Who Should Not Receive It

Responding to a query or comment that has come your way from someone else? If you do not mean to reply to everybody who has up to this point received the message, *do not use the "reply all" feature.*

Copying people unnecessarily, in this situation or any other, is

E-MAIL SELLING TECHNIQUES

a common breach of e-mail etiquette. One of the reasons that our e-mail boxes are overflowing—not the only reason, of course, but one of the reasons—is that we are sometimes far too eager to copy everyone who might conceivably have even a tangential connection with the message in question. If your query really is meant for the VP of Operations at BigCo, you should probably think twice before copying the CEO, the Board of Directors, every member of the Board of Directors, and every person on the sales staff. If nothing else, you will tick people off because they will assume you are always sending them messages they do not have to read—and they will be less likely to read the messages that really do relate to them. Use the "cc" field sparingly. (But do use it to keep key contacts, like the CEO, in the loop about your progress toward key goals—see Chapter 37.)

Mistake #18: Encouraging a Multiparty Shouting Match
When you are raising a controversial topic, and you have absolutely no option but to send a message to more than one person at a time, think hard about whether you really want everyone who reads your message to be able to respond to everyone else about what you've said.

Let me give you an example. If you have to pass along bad news about a delayed shipment, and you do not want to enable an online debate about the wisdom of deciding to work with your company in the first place, your best approach will be to avoid the "cc" field entirely. Instead, send the message to yourself and place all the relevant recipient e-mails in the "bcc," or "blind copy," field. This means that no one will be able to respond to the entire group by simply hitting "reply all." Anybody hitting reply will be addressing only you.

Mistake #19: Being (Perceived as) a Jerk
Here's the interesting thing about e-mail: It is extremely easy to misinterpret.

We, as readers of e-mail, lack any meaningful visual information from the sender. (We can't read body language or facial expressions the way we would in a real-life, one-to-one conversation.) Similarly, we as readers lack any information about the pitch or tone of the sender's intended "voice." (We can't hear whether the other person intends a remark to sound facetious, for instance.)

But to the writer, e-mail correspondence often feels very much like verbal communication—so much so that many people who "let it all hang out" while writing messages type out things that look strange, offensive, or even menacing in an e-mail message—but wouldn't draw a moment's notice if the same words were spoken casually. (Example: "You don't want to go there." Say it with a smile, and you're humorously changing the subject. Type it in an e-mail message, and it sounds like you're planning to send over a guy with brass knuckles.)

Bottom line: We as readers may come to the conclusion that somebody is being a jerk—while he or she does not realize the words chosen seem at all jerk-like.

So what do I really mean here? What I mean is, read your stuff over twice before you hit "send." Don't let the other person conclude that you are a jerk. In the world of e-mail, all it really takes to "be" a jerk is for you to inadvertently give someone the ammunition necessary to conclude that you are one. Stay away from sarcasm and irony; make sure nothing you've written could possibly be misconstrued.

Mistake #20: Mixing Business with Pleasure
This one is so obvious that many people miss it. Send business messages from your business e-mail—that is, from the one with your company's domain name at the end of it. Send personal messages from your personal e-mail address. Do not mix the two up. I know of people who maintain as many as five or six different e-mail addresses for different functions. That's fine, of course . . . as long as they keep everything in the right bucket.

Never, ever use your company's e-mail system to distribute personal communications.

Mistake #21: Rambling On and On
Even if your correspondent rambles on and on. the other person's long message to you is *not* permission to send a long message in return. If you think that *your* long message will be scanned reverently, as if it were a religious text, you have a fundamental misunderstanding of the job description behind the word *salesperson*.

If you really, truly cannot get the message across within the confines of a single screen of information, and you don't want to send an attachment, my suggestion is that you pick up the phone.

Mistake #22: Sending an E-mail Message in Anger

Never send an angry e-mail message to any business contact. At any time. Ever.

For professional salespeople, this is, quite simply, *never* a good idea. Take a break and come back to the message in an hour or two, after you've had the chance to calm down.

On Cold Calling

The Nine Principles of Cold Calling

Here are the nine proven principles that will support a successful cold calling campaign in virtually any industry. Follow them!

1. *Rather than set a daily "number-of-dials" goal, set the goal for the number of first appointments you want to maintain at all times.* As you learn more and more about your conversion ratios (see principle #3 below), make the adjustments that make sense for you to achieve your activity and income goals.

2. *Make cold calls daily with the objective of setting at least one new appointment every day.* This does not include networking meetings. Set a block of time to make calls for an uninterrupted period. Don't send e-mail or receive incoming calls during that time. Approach this activity with discipline and a sense of urgency.

3. *Begin tracking your dials, completed calls, and appointments set on a daily basis right now.* Compile your results daily; benchmark your activity to assess your success and help determine your true ratios.

4. *Do not stop dialing if you are not meeting with success.* Stand up, take a break, practice, reread this list of principles—do whatever you have to do, but don't stop. If you are calling within a particular industry and are finding it tough to set up appointments, diversify your leads.

5. *Always be prepared to make cold calls.* Have an identified lead list ready with you always; use it when you have unexpected time available. Don't let organizational issues get in your way. Do not research or prioritize your calls between calls—your calling time is your peak sales time! Do that work "off-peak."

6. *Learn the appropriate third-party references.* Briefly reference your company's past and current success stories—but don't let a lack of complete knowledge keep you from making calls. Don't promise you can do the same thing for this prospect as you did for the ABC Company. Instead, ask for a meeting so you can learn more about the person's unique situation and share what you did with ABC Company.

7. *Practice each aspect of the calling process until you are comfortable and confident with your approach.* Prepare for the specific objections you will hear; be more ready to turn them around than the other person is to brush you off. When in doubt, say, "You know, a lot of people told us that before they saw how we could. . . ."

8. *Ask directly for the appointment.* If you haven't asked for one meeting at one specific date and time during the course of the call, you aren't doing it right.

9. *Don't kid yourself.* Sales come from prospects, and prospects come from appointments.

For more information on improving your team's cold calling numbers, visit *www.dei-sales.com.*

Online Resources Worth Checking Out

Following is a small sampling of the e-mail marketing and newsletter resources you may wish to consult online.

ActionMessage—*www.ActionMessage.com*
activMailMan—*www.activmailman.com*
Admail.net—*www.admail.net*
Atomic Mail—*www.atomic-mail.com*
AtomPark Software—*www.amailsender.com*
AVI Mail—*www.avimail.com*
Aviatech—*www.aviatech.com*
Blizzard E-mail—*www.blizzardemail.com*
BlueHornet Networks—*www.bluehornet.com*
Bronto Software—*http://bronto.com*
Constant Contact—*www.constantcontact.com*
Customer Paradigm—*www.customerparadigm.com*
Customized Web Services—*http://customizedwebservices.com*
DocuMatix Email Manager—*www.documatix.com*
Dynamics Direct—*www.dynamicsdirect.com*
EDR—*www.edrplc.com*
eGOware—*www.egoware.com*
emailBlast—*www.emailblast.biz*
The Email Company—*www.theemailcompany.com*
Emailforms—*www.emailforms.com*
EmailLabs—*http://emaillabs.com*
E-mail Logic—*http://e-maillogic.com*
Email Marketing Central—*www.email-marketing-central.com*
Email-Marketing–Reports.com—*www.email-marketing-reports.com*
Email Marketing Software Solutions—*www.emailtools.co.uk*
EmailXtra.com—*www.emailxtra.com*
Endai Worldwide—*www.endai.com*
eNewsletter—*www.emailmarketingcampaign.com*
eNewsetter Pro—*www.enewsletterpro.com*
ennectMail—*www.ennectmail.com*
eProspecting (e-mail marketing for Realtors)—*www.eprospecting.com*
Equilibrix—*www.equilibrix.com*
eWayDirect—*www.ewaydirect.com*
ExactTarget—*http://exacttarget.com*
Ezemail—*www.ezemail.biz*

Global IntelliSystems—*www.globalintellisystems.com*
gravityMail—*www.gravitymail.com*
Harvest Digital—*www.harvestdigital.com*
Html Email Marketing—*www.html-email-marketing.com*
Inbox Interactive—*www.inboxinteractive.com*
INBOX Marketing—*www.inboxmarketinginc.com*
Info.now—*www.infonow-opt-in.com*
Interactive Marketing System—*www.interactivemarketingsystem.com*
Internet Mail Manager—*www.Internetmailmanager.com*
iPost.com—*www.ipost.com*
iRealty—*www.irealty.com.au*
Lencom Software—*www.lencom.com*
List Sorcerer—*www.listsorcerer.com*
Listrak—*www.listrak.com*
M4Internet—*www.m4Internet.com*
Mailout.com—*www.mailout.com*
Mailtube Email Marketing—*www.mailtube.co.uk*
Market Wire—*http://marketwire.com*
My Mail Genie—*www.mymailgenie.com*
NetHawk Interactive—*www.nethawk.net*
NewsGoodies—*http://newsgoodies.com*
NewsletterPro—*www.newsletterpro.com*
NextMark—*www.nextmark.com*
nTarget—*www.ntarget.com*
Onletterhead—*www.onletterhead.com*
Online Email Marketing—*www.mailgenie.biz*
Online-Marketers—*www.online-marketers.net*
PR Newswire—*http://prnewswire.com*
Profit Smart DM Software—*www.profitsmartdm.com*
Pure—*www.pure360.com*
Pure Reach—*www.purereach.com*
ResultsMail—*www.resultsmail.com*
Rich E-mail Marketing—*www.richemailmarketing.com*
Satori Software—*www.satorisoftware.co.uk*
Sevista eMarketing Technology—*www.sevista.com*
SmartMail—*www.smartmail.co.nz*
Sourcekit Email Manager—*http://emailmanager.sourcekit.com*
SubscriberMail—*www.subscribermail.com*
Touchpoint Energized Communications—*www.touchpointec.com*
Tugnut—*www.tugnut.com*
VastCast Media—*www.vastcastmedia.com*
VerticalResponse—*www.verticalresponse.com*
VIBEdirect—*www.vibedirect.com*
WindyMail—*www.windymail.com*

Index

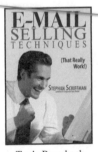

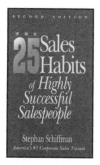

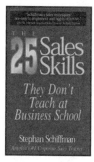

About the Author

Stephan Schiffman is president of D.E.I. Management Group, Inc., one of the largest sales training companies in the U.S. He is the author of a number of best-selling books including *Cold Calling Techniques (That Really Work!)*; *The 25 Most Common Sales Mistakes*; *The 25 Habits of Highly Successful Salespeople*; *Beat Sales Burnout*; *Ask Questions, Get Sales*; *Telesales*; *Closing Techniques (That Really Work!)*; and *The #1 Sales Team*. Schiffman's articles have appeared in *The Wall Street Journal*, *The New York Times* and *INC. Magazine*. He has also appeared as a guest on CNBC's *Minding Your Business*, *How to Succeed in Business*, and *Smart Money*. For more information about Stephan Schiffman, and D.E.I. Management, call 1-800-224-2140 or visit *www.dei-sales.com*.